# HEALTHY
# INDIAN COOKING

# HEALTHY
# INDIAN COOKING

SHEHZAD HUSAIN

PHOTOGRAPHS BY JAMES MURPHY

SERIES EDITOR
LEWIS ESSON

STEWART, TABORI & CHANG
NEW YORK

First published in 1997 by Frances Lincoln Limited
4 Torriano Mews
Torriano Avenue
London, NW5 2RZ England

Text copyright © Shehzad Husain 1997
Photographs copyright © James Murphy 1997

Published in 1998 and distributed by
Stewart, Tabori & Chang,
a division of U.S. Media Holdings, Inc.
115 West 18th Street, New York, NY 10011

Distributed in Canada by
General Publishing Company Ltd
30 Lesmill Road
Don Mills, Ontario, M3B 2T6, Canada

The author has asserted her moral rights.

Library of Congress Catalog Card Number:
97–68926

ISBN 1 55670 679 0

Printed and bound in Hong Kong

1 3 5 7 9 10 8 6 4 2

# CONTENTS

# INTRODUCTION

With its emphasis on nutritious vegetables, legumes, rice, and grains, the traditional cooking of India and Pakistan has always been, by its very nature, healthy. The meat and dairy products so dominant in Western cooking play a much more subsidiary role, almost as flavoring elements rather than building blocks, which means that saturated fat levels are—or should be—much lower.

I say "should be" as there is one aspect of our tradition which tends to boost saturated fat levels and that is the use of ghee (clarified butter, see page 29) as the favored cooking medium, and often even as a dressing poured over legume dishes like dhals. Generally throughout this book, however, I have replaced it with healthier vegetable or olive oil, and although flavors will not be exactly the same I think the only area in which this might be obvious is in the making of bread (see Naan, page 124).

The inventive and imaginative use of spices also means that you can normally sacrifice more caloric ingredients (spices are almost entirely calorie-free!) without much noticeable loss of flavor. You will also find, as you experiment with the addition of spices to your food, that you will not need to add so much salt in your cooking.

Aromatics such as garlic, ginger, and turmeric, whole grains and oil-rich nuts and seeds, as well as vegetables such as spinach, pumpkin, and sweet potatoes, are all now vaunted as "superfoods," not only blessed with ample nutrients but containing agents that actively combat disease. These ingredients are at the heart of Indian cooking, making it both immensely flavorful and incredibly healthy.

**EATING IN THE SUBCONTINENT**

Among the questions I am most frequently asked by Westerners about Indian and Pakistani food is exactly what constitutes a typical meal and how is it served.

In my experience a typical main meal for four consists of one meat, chicken, or fish dish, with one vegetarian dish or dhal dish, a rice dish, and some form of bread. These would also be accompanied by a raita (yogurt relish) and an assortment of chutneys or pickles. Obviously the ideal is an assortment of dishes that marry well in terms of flavor and texture (and color). If, for example, the meat dish is a dry one, aim to serve a vegetable dish with lots of sauce.

Of course, this is a meal typical of a household of meat-eaters; the equivalent in a vegetarian household might consist of one or more vegetarian curries, one dhal or other legume dish (essential as the principal source of protein), and a raita (again essential), together with a rice dish and bread, and a small assortment of chutneys in the same way.

When entertaining, there would obviously be a much wider array of dishes on offer—several meat, chicken, and fish or shellfish dishes, two or three vegetarian dishes and dhals or other legume dishes, with plenty of rice and bread, and as wide a range of accompaniments as you could manage. This would normally be followed by a couple of desserts: one of the traditional Indian desserts alongside a fruit salad or simply an assortment of fresh fruit.

Unless otherwise stated, all the recipes in this book have been planned on the basis that each will form part of a typical Indian or Pakistani meal, where four people will share four or five different dishes plus rice, bread, and accompaniments in the manner described above. If you are planning to cook for more or fewer people, you are best advised to make more or fewer dishes (with a minimum of three), rather than scale the recipes up or down.

## A FEW NOTES ON TECHNIQUES

There are very few difficult or unusual techniques involved in this book. However, the following do warrant a little bit of extra information.

### GRINDING SPICES

As I say later in my guide to ingredients, although ready-ground spices are a great convenience, nothing quite matches the aroma and taste of spices ground yourself as you need them. If you start doing this, you will notice the marked effect in the fuller, richer, and deeper flavors.

Fairly inexpensive little electric spice grinders are now widely available, or many people use coffee grinders (but it is not a good idea to use the same one for both spices and coffee as you do tend to get flavor transfer, even if you keep the machine scrupulously clean). However, I have to admit that I much prefer the good old-fashioned method of pulverizing the spices using a pestle and mortar.

You do get a coarser product this way, but I think the bruising process of a pestle and mortar retains more of the flavoring elements than is the case when the spices are blitzed to a powder. If the spices are going to be given quite lengthy cooking they don't need to be ground too finely, as any larger particles will be softened before they are eaten. If, however, the dish for which they are required is, say, a rapid stir-fry, then it is wiser to grind finely or you may end up with a gritty texture.

### ROASTING SPICES, SEEDS, AND NUTS

As you will see in the recipes, whole spices, seeds, and nuts are often first roasted, as this develops their flavors. In India this would be done on a thawa (see below), but it is very easy to do in a dry nonstick frying pan. The pan is placed over a moderate heat and the spices, seeds, or nuts stirred continuously, or the pan tilted and shaken to ensure even cooking, until the items being roasted are well colored and aromatic. Particularly when dealing with oily seeds and nuts, you do have to keep a careful eye on the contents of the pan as they can burn very quickly if left too long over the heat.

### STIR-FRYING

Although stir-frying is generally more associated with Chinese cooking, you will see that I make considerable use of the technique as it keeps a higher proportion of the nutrients (and flavor and texture) of ingredients. The technique could not be easier to master, but it is surprising how alien some Western cooks find its principles and practice.

In general all that you have to remember is that the ingredients are added in stages, grouping together at each stage all those items that will take the same time to cook, so that at the end of the process everything is cooked to the right degree at the same time. This can mean, however, that there are no obvious visual signs of when you have reached the right stage to add the next batch of ingredients as what is in the pan is still in the process of cooking, so you have to use your instincts and learn from experience.

Preparation is critical in stir-frying. Get all your ingredients peeled and chopped before you start cooking. (Don't do this too far ahead or you will lose freshness and nutrients.) It helps to group together—say, in separate bowls—the ingredients that are going to be added at each stage. Also cut each ingredient into pieces that are roughly the same size, so they will cook uniformly.

As you will see, I usually start the process by stir-frying the flavoring ingredients, such as spices, for less than a minute until they are aromatic, before I add anything else. However, I may also add chopped or sliced onion at this early stage as onions usually need to be cooked until they are quite soft.

Often very delicate items, like green leaves or fresh herbs, are added at the very last minute and stirred in briefly merely to wilt them before the dish is served.

For the actual method of frying, it is best to stir the contents of the pan in repeated sweeping backward and forward semi-circular movements to ensure that all the food in contact with the bottom of the pan is stirred up to prevent it catching.

## SOME USEFUL UTENSILS

### THAWA

This round, slightly concave iron plate or griddle is used for making breads like chapatis. A good, heavy, nonstick frying pan will give perfectly good results.

### KADAHI

This pan is very similar to a wok, although slightly heavier and with a ring-shaped handle on either side. A wok or a good, heavy, deepish frying pan will work well in its place.

## SOME NOTES ON NUTRITION

The figures given in the nutritional information panel that accompanies each recipe are per serving and have been rounded off to the nearest whole number. Optional ingredients have not been included and the figures are based on the largest number of suggested servings.

The percentage of the total calories in each dish contributed by fat is given in brackets after the total fat figure per serving. Please note that this figure can occasionally produce results that seem surprising when not viewed in a wider context. For example, a salad or dhal made with only 2 tablespoons of oil can have a very low overall calorie count, so its fat content reads as a fairly high percentage. However, were that salad or dhal to be analyzed with an accompanying bowl of rice, the increase in total calories could reduce the level of fat to a medium, or even low, percentage.

# SOME INDIAN INGREDIENTS

**SPICES**

Nothing characterizes Indian cooking more than its vivid and imaginative use of dried spices, possibly because so many of the plants from which the spices are derived are either native to the subcontinent or grow there well. Indeed, India is now the world's largest exporter of spices.

Of course, "spicy" doesn't have to mean "hot." Just as salt and pepper levels are adjusted to suit personal taste in European cooking, the quantities of salt and chilies in Indian and Pakistani cuisine may be varied without in any way compromising the authenticity of the dish—don't let anyone bully you into eating or using quantities of chili that you find so excessive that you cannot really sense, let alone enjoy, the flavors underlying them.

USING SPICES

There are many ways of employing spices. You can use them whole, ground, roasted, fried, or mixed with yogurt to marinate meat and poultry. One spice can completely alter the flavor of a dish and combinations of several in varying proportions can produce totally different colors and textures.

Many of the recipes in this book call for ground spices, which are generally available in supermarkets as well as in Indian and Pakistani food shops. In India, we almost always buy whole spices and grind them ourselves, and there is no doubt that freshly ground spices do make a noticeable difference in taste. However, it cannot be denied that it is more convenient and quicker to use ready-ground spices.

Always buy spices from a store that has a rapid turnover, otherwise you may end up with old spices that have lost all their flavor—or developed a mustiness or off-flavor that will actually mar any dish in which they are used. Ready-ground spices, in particular, only have a shelf-life of a few months. Keep all spices in tightly closed jars in a cool, dry place away from sunlight (spice racks of clear bottles sitting on windowsills are not a good idea).

For some of the recipes in this book, the spices need to be roasted. In India this is done on a thawa, but you can also use a heavy, ideally cast-iron, frying pan or skillet. Do not add any water or oil to the spices; simply dry-roast them whole until lightly colored and highly aromatic, shaking the pan continuously to prevent burning.

AMCHOOR *Mangifera indica*

Also known as mango powder and sometimes spelled *amchur*, this flavoring, popular in North and East India, is made from unripe mangoes that have been sliced and sun-dried. It is mainly used to impart a tart fruity sourness to fish and vegetable dishes, although it also appears in some breads and pastries. It is sometimes sprinkled on meat and poultry to tenderize them. Mangoes are regarded as system cleansers and as kidney tonics.

CARDAMOM *Elettaria cardamomum, Elaichi*

Native to the tropical jungles of southern India, cardamom is probably the second most expensive spice, after saffron. The pods can be used with or without their husks and have a slightly pungent but very aromatic taste. They come in three varieties: green, white, and black. The green and white pods (the white are green pods that have been bleached for the sake of appearance) can be used for both sweet and savory dishes or to flavor rice. The black, which are not true cardamom but from plants of the related *Amomum* and *Afromomum* genus, are cheaper, coarser, and less aromatic, and are only used for savory dishes.

Cardamom's essential oils are particularly volatile, so it is better to buy the intact pods and use them whole, where appropriate, or crush them for the inner seeds as required.

In the subcontinent cardamom pods are chewed as breath fresheners and digestive aids, and they are also said to sharpen the mind.

### CHILI *Capsicum frutescens*

Dried red chilies (*sabath sookhi laal mirch*) are sold whole in some supermarkets and in most Asian stores. They are extremely fiery and should be used with caution; their effect can be toned down slightly by slitting them open and shaking out the seeds. Dried chilies are usually fried in oil before use. When handling dried chilies be careful not to touch any sensitive parts of your body—or of anyone else's—and wash your hands immediately afterwards. Crushed dried chilies, usually known as red pepper flakes, are also sold, but tend to be less potent and flavorful than the whole pods. Chili powder (*laal mirch*) and cayenne pepper can be very fiery when fresh, but have less potency than crushed dried red pepper flakes.

### CINNAMON *Cinnamomum verum, Dhalchini*

This most warming and familiar of spices is made from the bark of a tree of the laurel family that is native to Sri Lanka. It is sold as sticks, which are actually quills of rolled bark, and in powder form. When I use whole sticks I like to leave them in for serving as they look attractive; if your guests are unfamiliar with Indian food, however, do warn them that the cinnamon should not be eaten. Cinnamon is held to be a natural system cleanser and an aid to digestion. It is also antibacterial and helps relieve congestion.

### CLOVES *Eugenia caryophylus, Laung*

Cloves are the dried unopened flower buds of a small evergreen tree native to the Moluccas, or Spice Islands, now part of Indonesia. Cloves lend a warming pungency to many sweet and savory dishes and are usually added whole in Indian cooking. Like cinnamon sticks, they are often removed after cooking (hence the common European practice of studding onions with cloves so that they are then easier to remove). The spike of a whole clove is sometimes also used to secure a rolled betel leaf for serving as a breath freshener after an Indian meal. Look for cloves that have paler crowns than spikes and that snap cleanly, possibly exuding a little oil when pressed. Ground cloves form part of most garam masala mixtures (see opposite). The essential oil from cloves has long been used as a natural painkiller, particularly against toothaches. It also aids digestion and relieves flatulence.

### CORIANDER SEEDS *Coriandrum sativum, Dhania*

The aromatic brown seeds of the coriander plant have a pungent, slightly lemony flavor and are widely used in meat, fish, and poultry dishes. They are available whole, coarsely ground, and powdered. The ground versions lose their potency very quickly.

Try to buy Indian coriander seeds, which are sweeter,

paler and more elongated than more readily available Moroccan seeds. Coriander seeds are noted for their beneficial effect on the digestive system.

### CUMIN *Cuminum cyminum*

There are two main varieties of cumin seeds: the more common light brown type and the black. The smaller, thinner black cumin seeds (*shah zeera*), native to India and Pakistan, have a stronger and sweeter aromatic flavor, almost akin to caraway. Used to flavor curries and rice, they are available from most good Asian stores, but do tend to be more expensive than ordinary cumin. The flavor of cumin, like that of most seeds, is greatly improved by roasting or frying prior to use. Ground cumin (*safaid zeera*) has a musty smell and is widely used for flavoring lentils and vegetable curries. It is also an important ingredient in most curry powders and in garam masala (see right).

### FENNEL SEEDS *Foeniculum vulgare, Sonfe*

Very similar in appearance to white cumin, these seeds have a sweet aniseed taste and are used to flavor some curries and many vegetarian and fish dishes. They can also be chewed (like betel leaves and cardamom) after a spicy meal. Fennel seeds are said to help the body digest fatty foods and also help to suppress the appetite.

### FENUGREEK *Trigonella foenum-graecum, Methi*

The flavor of the whole dried flat yellow seeds is almost unpalatably astringent, but improves, when the seeds are lightly fried, to that of a slightly bitter celery or lovage. Ground fenugreek seeds are an ingredient in many curry powders and, as they are relatively cheap, tend to predominate in poorer-quality blends. Rich in vitamin A, fenugreek is noted for its ability to cleanse the body of toxins.

### GARAM MASALA

Meaning "hot spices," these aromatic mixtures of spices can either be made at home from freshly ground spices or bought ready-made. There is no set formula, but a typical mixture might include black cumin seeds, peppercorns, cloves, cinnamon, and black cardamom seeds.

To make your own, gently roast in a dry frying pan over moderate heat until aromatic a 1-inch piece of cinnamon stick with 3 cloves, 3 black peppercorns, the seeds from 2 black cardamom pods, and 2 teaspoons black cumin seeds. Allow to cool, then grind together. If you wish, multiply the quantities, grind, and store in an airtight jar for future use.

If buying commercial ready-made garam masala, note that the pastes keep their potency longer than the powders. Garam masala tends to be added at a fairly late stage in cooking, or even as a garnish, in order to get the most benefit from the aroma of the spices.

GINGER *Zingiber officinale, Sonth*
Ground dried ginger as well as fresh ginger are used in Indian cooking. Both are readily available in most supermarkets.

MUSTARD SEEDS *Brassica nigra, B. juncea, Sarson ke beenji rai*
These seeds, either black or yellow, are round and sharp-flavored. They are used to flavor curries and pickles and develop a delicious nutty taste when first fried in oil. Mustard seeds stimulate the appetite and are said to be good for the skin.

NUTMEG *Mystica fragrans, Jaifal*
Nutmeg is the dried kernel of the fruit of a flowering evergreen tree native to the Moluccas. Its rich, sweet, warm, and aromatic flavor is quite fugitive, so try to avoid the ready-ground powders and grate whole nutmegs as you need them. Nutmeg is traditionally thought to have general tonic properties, especially for the digestive system, heart, brain, and reproductive organs.

ONION SEEDS *Allium cepa, Kalongi*
Black in color and triangular in shape, these seeds are used to flavor both pickles and vegetable curries.

PAPRIKA *Capsicum tetragonum*
This powder, made from dried varieties of sweet red peppers, (mostly pericarps), was, until recently, thought of in the West as a hot-flavored spice but is very mild in comparison to chili pepper. There are sweet and hot varieties of the powder, usually depending on whether or not the peppers' seeds have been included. Ubiquitous in the cuisines of Spain and Eastern Europe, paprika is occasionally used in Indian cooking.

PEPPERCORNS *Piper nigrum*
The peppercorn is one of the oldest spices known to humankind and is native to the tropical forests of India's Malabar Coast. After salt, pepper is probably the most common flavoring in both Western and Indian cooking. Peppercorns are the tiny berries of a vining shrub; they are picked when fully developed but still unripe.

Black peppercorns are sun-dried; white peppercorns are first soaked in water so that the outer skin may be washed off to reveal the pale inner core prior to sun-drying. As the flavor is mostly held in the outer skin, while the pungency lies in the inner core, white pepper is "hotter" than black but with a more subtle flavor. It is often favored in dishes with pale sauces, to avoid speckling.

Green peppercorns (*badi mirch*) are the freshly harvested berries and are usually preserved either in vinegar or brine, although they may be freeze-dried or commercially dehydrated. They have a much fresher, almost caper-like, flavor.

Red or pink peppercorns come from a totally unrelated plant, the Brazilian pepper (*Schinus terebinthifolius*). These have little pungency but a sweet citrusy flavor and look highly decorative. Mixtures of all four types of peppercorns are available and give an interesting blend of flavors and pungency.

Pepper stimulates the appetite and digestion, encourages perspiration, and also has considerable antioxidant and antibacterial properties.

POMEGRANATE SEEDS *Punica granatum, Anar dana*
It is said that the fruit with which Eve tempted Adam in the Garden of Eden was not an apple at all, but a pomegranate, and its name can be translated as "apple with seeds." The fruit and its seeds are a potent symbol of fertility in many cultures. The fresh seeds of the fruit are a popular garnish in Middle Eastern cooking and the dried seeds,

resembling small raisins, are valued for their sweet-and-sour flavor in Indian cooking. Ground dried pomegranate seeds are used as a souring agent in Northern Indian cooking, particularly in their chutneys and vegetable and legume dishes.

### Poppy Seeds *Papaver somniferum, Khush khush*

These are the dried seeds of the opium poppy; although opium is derived from the unripe seed pod, the seeds do not contain any of the drug. Seeds of the variety common in India are yellow in color as opposed to the blue-gray of the seeds so long familiar in the West. Their delicious nutty flavor is always better when they have first been roasted. They are used, often whole, to flavor curries. Ground poppy seeds are sometimes used as a thickening agent.

### Saffron *Crocus sativus, Zafran*

The world's most expensive spice, saffron is made from the stigmas of the saffron crocus, which is native to Asia Minor. The production of each ounce of saffron requires around five thousand stigmas, and each crocus bears only three stigmas, which need to be hand-picked at precisely the right stage of development. Fortunately, only a small quantity of saffron is needed to flavor or color a dish, whether sweet or savory. Saffron is sold both as whole threads and in powder form. It has a beautiful flavor and fragrance. To bring out the flavor, saffron is often first very lightly roasted and then soaked in milk. Beware of poor-quality or adulterated saffron, which can have a disagreeably bitter flavor.

### Sesame Seeds *Sesamum indicum, Thill*

The flat, cream-colored unhulled seeds of an Asian and African annual, sesame seeds have been cultivated since antiquity for their abundant oil. Their full nutty flavor is best developed by roasting, and they are used to flavor some curries. Use bright-looking seeds; older seeds in which the oils have gone rancid develop a muddy gray appearance.

### Tamarind *Tamarindus indica, Imli*

The tamarind plant, also known as the Indian date, grows freely in India, and its dried black pods are sticky and very sour-tasting. Their sweet-and-sour fruity flavor is very familiar to Westerners as the basis for Worcestershire sauce. In India it is used in many curries, especially with lentils and vegetables, and chutneys. Tamarind has to be soaked in hot water to extract the flavor. Lemon juice, though much weaker, is often used as a substitute. Nowadays tamarind can be bought in paste form in jars. Mix the paste with a little water to get it to a runny consistency before use. Tamarind is noted for its mild laxative effect.

### Turmeric *Curcuma longa, Haled*

The turmeric plant is related to ginger and, as with ginger, it is the rhizome, or underground stem, that is valued for its flavor. Seldom available fresh in the West, it is usually sold dried and most commonly ground. The bitter-tasting spice is used mainly for its bright yellow color (often as a cheap substitute for saffron) rather than its flavor, although its musky taste is important in most curry powders. It has significant powers to aid digestion and as an antiseptic and antifungal, and is often used to treat wounds. Be careful when working with it as it stains very easily.

## HERBS

Perhaps because of the overwhelmingly powerful presence of spices in Indian food—and the long cooking that these often need to develop flavor—herbs are not nearly as important in Indian cooking as they are in Western cooking, or even in the neighboring Southeast Asian cuisines.

Nevertheless, several herbs are fairly common in Indian cooking, principally because they marry well with other frequently used ingredients.

BAY LEAVES *Laurus nobilis, Tez patta*
One of the most ancient of herbs used in cooking, the leaves of the bay or laurel tree are sold fresh and dried. Although the crushed dried leaves are sometimes included in garam masala mixtures, bay is not very widely used in curries.

CILANTRO *Coriandrum sativum, Hara dhania*
This beautifully fragrant herb is used in Indian cooking much as parsley is in the West, both as an ingredient and as a garnish. Its zesty flavor marries well with chilies, and for

this reason it has been adopted in most cuisines in which chilies also feature. I must admit to being an addict, and you will see that it features in most of my savory recipes.

Until recently cilantro was relatively difficult to find in the West. In appearance it is fairly similar to flat-leafed parsley, though cilantro is often sold with its roots intact, as these and the stems are useful for flavoring stocks and vegetable and pulse dishes. If you are having difficulty differentiating between cilantro and parsley, rub a leaf between two fingers; the aroma released on the fingers will make the difference obvious.

CURRY LEAVES *Murraya koenigii, Kari patta*
These are similar in appearance to bay leaves but very different in flavor, with a distinct curry-like aroma. They can be bought both dried and occasionally fresh (unfortunately, the dried leaves have considerably less flavor than the fresh) and are used principally to flavor lentil dishes and vegetable curries.

FENUGREEK *Trigonella foenum-graecum, Methi*
Fresh fenugreek, sold in bunches, has very small leaves and is used to flavor both meat and vegetarian dishes. The dried leaves are also used.

MINT *Mentha* spp., *Podina*
The fresh taste of mint leaves has long been appreciated in India, especially in lamb dishes, chutneys, and raitas. It also works very well in tandem with cilantro. Dried mint leaves don't seem to retain much of the power of the fresh, one reason why I favor commercial mint sauces as a flavoring if fresh leaves are not available.

## OTHER AROMATICS

These fresh vegetables are mostly used like herbs and spices, for their flavoring properties.

As ginger and garlic are used very frequently in curries, and it takes time and effort to peel and chop them, I suggest you take about 8 ounces of each, soak them overnight (this makes them easier to peel), peel them, and grind them separately in a food processor, adding a little water to form a pulp. They can then be stored in airtight containers in the refrigerator for about a month.

Alternatively, for the recipes in which I specify a teaspoon of garlic or ginger pulp, you can substitute two finely chopped garlic cloves or one shredded half-inch slice of ginger. There are also good-quality commercial ginger and garlic sauces that deliver much of the flavor of these aromatics with little or no effort, and I do use them when cooking in a hurry or with no chance of advance preparation.

CHILIES *Capsicum frutescens*
Fresh green chilies (*hari mirch*) and their riper red counterparts are used in Indian cooking as both an ingredient and a garnish. As well as imparting their own richly aromatic flavor and their heat, they also have the power to bring out the flavors of the ingredients around them. Originally from South America, chilies are now mostly grown in Africa and Indonesia. Look for crisp and firm peppers, with no wrinkles or blemishes.

Those used to the pungency of chilies tend to cook the entire pepper, even when chopped or sliced. In this book I only specify seeding chilies where I think it is necessary. However, those not as accustomed to chili heat ought to remove the seeds and the pale membrane to which they are attached, as these are the hottest parts. As with dried peppers, take great care when handling peppers not to touch the face and other sensitive parts of the body, and remember to wash your hands well immediately afterwards.

Fresh chilies are packed with vitamins A, B, and C (in fact, pound for pound, they are six times richer in vitamin C than oranges). They are also potent stimulants to the system and highly antibacterial. They are also proven to help normalize blood pressure.

### GARLIC *Allium sativum, Lassun*

The garlic plant is a member of the lily family, and its bulbs, or heads, have been used to flavor food since ancient times. Garlic is frequently used in curries, especially in conjunction with ginger, and whole cloves of it are sometimes added to lentil dishes. Garlic powder is useful for adding to flour to make a spicy coating for food.

As long as garlic has been known it has been valued as much for its medicinal properties as for its flavor, and today it is hailed as one of the "superfoods" with active health-giving properties. It is antiseptic and powerfully antibacterial when raw, and even when cooked it helps the body eliminate toxins and lowers cholesterol.

### GINGER *Zingiber officinale, Adrak*

Although fresh ginger is sometimes called gingerroot, the part of the plant that is used to flavor food is actually a rhizome, or thickened underground stem. Fresh ginger is one of the most popular and ancient of flavorings used in India and is an important ingredient in many curries. For Indian dishes, ginger is usually peeled and then cut into matchstick shreds, or used as a pulp (see page 17).

Ginger is a potent stimulant and aids the digestive processes. Research has also shown that it is effective in reducing the nausea associated with travel sickness and vertigo and it has, indeed, been a folk treatment for these ailments for centuries. Infusions of ginger are also recommended for colds and sore throats.

## VEGETABLES

### CAULIFLOWER *Phool gobi*

This close relative of the cabbage and broccoli is a favorite of Indian vegetarian cooking because of its fine texture and ability to absorb other flavors. Like cabbage, cauliflower must not be overcooked or it starts to break down and give off a sulfurous odor. Buy only fresh-looking cauliflowers with firm curds, ideally still with unwilted leaves attached. Many people go for a perfect white color; but, in fact, the greenish varieties cook faster and are often more flavorful. Like all members of the cabbage family, the cauliflower is rich in the antioxidants that help prevent cancer. It is also richer in calcium and folic acid than almost any other vegetable, so earning itself the epithet "vegetable liver."

### DOODHI *Lagenaria siceria*

Also known as *lokhi,* or bottle gourd, this smooth pale green variety of gourd, reminiscent of a large cucumber, is very important in the cooking of India. The firm but tender flesh of young specimens is very flavorful, with hints of cucumber and zucchini, but they do become unpleasantly bitter and tough when old. They are usually peeled before use and any large seeds removed.

### EGGPLANT *Baingun, Brinjal*

Eggplant, a member of the same family as the potato and the tomato, is much favored in the vegetarian cooking of its native India because of its adaptability, fine meaty texture, and ability to absorb and blend strong added flavors.

Look for well-rounded specimens with taut, unwrinkled, and unblemished skins. Leave the skins on; they are quite digestible and highly nutritious. Eggplant is rich in bioflavinoids, which help arterial renewal and prevent blood clotting. It is also thought to help prevent some forms of cancer.

### GREEN BEAN *Sem*

There are literally hundreds of varieties of green beans (*Phaseolus vulgaris*) cultivated all over the world; though they may vary in color and dimension, they all have much the same characteristics. Generally the firmer and brighter they are the better, and they should snap cleanly and crisply when broken (hence their alternative name "snap beans"). They need to be topped and tailed prior to cooking. Most varieties now sold have been bred to be stringless, but if you encounter some types that have tough strings these must also be removed. Brief preliminary blanching also helps fix the beans' bright color.

### MOOLI

Also known as daikon, this large pale radish looks more like a big smooth parsnip and has a wonderful sharp peppery flavor. It is also much richer in vitamin C than the little red radishes common in the West. Buy only firm moolis that seem heavy for their size; they keep well for some time in the refrigerator, so don't worry about buying one that is bigger than you need for one dish. They are also excellent aids to the digestion, particularly of starchy foods like pulses and potatoes, and thought to help prevent cancer.

### OKRA *Bhindi*

Also known as ladies' fingers, these are the immature seedpods of a small bush related to the cotton plant and native to Africa. When fresh, they have a wonderful rich flavor and are filled with edible seeds in a mucilaginous liquid that acts as a natural thickening agent. Look for smallish firm glossy pods with no hints of browning at the tips. If using them whole, be careful when removing the stalk end not to break into the interior of the pod or you will lose the liquid. Okra is highly nutritious, rich in vegetable protein and folic acid, and the liquid is believed to soothe the digestive tract.

### SPINACH *Saag*

Rather than the common spinach (*Spinacea oleracea*) familiar in the West, the leaves used in India are most likely to be from a member of the unrelated mallow family, Malabar Nightshade (*Basella alba* and *B. rubra*). They are very similar, so the two can be used interchangeably. Although highly nutritious—it is particularly rich in vitamin A and minerals (especially iron and calcium)—spinach is also high in oxalic acid. When cooked, this has the effect of inhibiting the body's absorption of some nutrients, so avoid eating too much cooked spinach at one sitting or having it as part of several meals in succession.

SWEET POTATO *Ipomoea batatas, Shakar kand*

These tubers of a member of the convolvulus family native to Central America are now grown all over the tropics. There are several varieties with yellowish, pinkish, red, or purple skins, but they fall into two main types: one with drier mealier yellowish flesh and one with softer more moist white flesh. The latter have a sweeter flavor and are more popular in Asia. They are cooked much like potatoes, mostly boiled or baked in their skins. Choose plump specimens with unwrinkled skins. Sweet potatoes are highly nutritious and easily digested. They are believed to be good for the circulation and to help eliminate toxins.

## LEGUMES AND DHALS

BLACK-EYED PEAS *Lobhia*

These cream-colored beans get their name from the irregular black spot along their stem ends. They boast a fine buttery texture and a nutty, smoky flavor, cook quickly, and require no presoaking. High in protein, black-eyed peas are an important food in India.

CHICKPEAS *Chhole*

These irregularly shaped buff-colored peas look a little like hazelnuts, have a full nutty flavor, and keep their shape well when cooked. Chickpeas do, however, need long soaking

and cooking times, after which the outer skins have to be removed. Fortunately, the readily available canned chickpeas, which require no work, have quite a good flavor and an excellent texture (and retain a considerable amount of nutrients). In India, roasted dried chickpeas (*bhoonay chanay*) are sold as a snack.

### KIDNEY BEANS *Rajma*

There is a wide variety of these highly nutritious beans, all of which keep their shape and buttery texture well when cooked. All members of this family, however, contain toxins in the skin that need to be eliminated by boiling rapidly for 10-15 minutes  before simmering slowly until tender. As with chickpeas, canned red kidney beans have a good flavor and texture and retain a substantial percentage of their nutrients.

### CHANA DHAL

Very similar in appearance to yellow split peas, with slightly less shiny grains, chana dhal is actually a variety of chickpea. It has a sweet "meaty" flavor and accounts for about fifty percent of the pulse crop in the subcontinent. If you can't find chana dhal at Indian or Pakistani grocers, substitute yellow split peas.

### MASOOR DHAL

These small, round, salmon-colored split lentils, which turn yellow when cooked, are stocked by many supermarkets, labeled simply "lentils" or "red lentils." Lentils require no presoaking, but do need to be picked over carefully prior to cooking to remove any stones or other debris. Lentils are highly nutritious and easily digested.

### MOONG DHAL

These teardrop-shaped yellow split lentils are more popular in northern India than in the south.

### TOOR DHAL

This small orangey-red legume, also known as *tur* or *arhar*, is the pigeon pea. It is almost exclusively used in the south and west of India as it will usually not grow in the colder north. It is very popular as it is light, easy to cook and highly digestible.

### URID DHAL

Though very similar in shape and size to moong dhal, these lentils are white and a little drier when cooked. As with moong dhal, they are more popular among northern Indians.

## FRUIT

### GUAVA *Amrood*

This pearlike fruit of a tree of the myrtle family is native to the Americas but is now found all over the world, growing in both tropical and subtropical areas. The aroma of the grainy flesh is reminiscent of quince, but with a sweet-and-sour exoticism that produces memorable sorbets, fruit butters, and jams. Look for large guavas with a pleasing floral scent (overripe guavas tend to have an overpowering aroma) and a pale skin that gives slightly to gentle pressure. The guava is said to be good for the bones and for the lymphatic system.

### MANGO *Aam*

A good well-ripened mango ranks among the most delicious of fruits, and it is no accident that a gift of mangoes is a symbol of friendship in India. Unfortunately, all too often mangoes sold in the West have been picked too early (and may never ripen) or are of a variety that is naturally fibrous and may even possess a flavor that hints of paint thinner. You have to be very picky—even when buying green unripe fruit for cooking—and should be prepared to pay a little extra; after all, good mangoes are expensive even in the places where they are grown. Buy heavy firm fruit that just yields to pressure and has a fine perfumed scent, with no hint of fermentation in it.

To cut the flesh from a ripe mango, cut down through the fruit lengthwise on either side of the pit. Take the two half-round sections you have removed and cut a lattice into the flesh, then press the outside of the curved skins to turn these sections inside out, producing easily removable cubes of flesh on the other side. Any flesh still clinging to the pit may be sliced off, or nibbled off as a treat. Mangoes are regarded as great systemic cleansers, good for the skin and for the kidneys.

### PAPAYA *Papai*

Also known as pawpaw, the papaya is native to the tropical Americas but came to India before the end of the sixteenth century. As the trees are particularly generous bearers, they are an important part of the economy (second only to bananas) in many tropical areas. This large oval or pear-shaped fruit resembles melon. Its perfumed orangey-yellow flesh is delicious when ripe, and the black seeds have a peppery flavor and are often used as a condiment or garnish. As with mangoes, unripe papayas are sometimes cooked like vegetables. Again, buy fruit that feels heavy for its size, that is just beginning to soften, and that bears no trace of green on the skin. Papayas are rich in the enzyme papain, which breaks down proteins, so they are used as a meat tenderizer and in marinades. This means that they can also help in the digestion of a protein-rich meal. Papaya has considerable powers as a general cleanser and detoxifier. It is said to keep the eyes and skin bright, and some people use the juice to try to remove freckles.

### PINEAPPLE *Ananas*

After the banana, the pineapple is probably the most familiar of tropical fruits in the West. Indeed, the pine-cone-shaped fruit has been a popular decorative device in Europe for centuries. Native to the West Indies, pineapple is now grown all over the tropics, including Hawaii, the largest producer.

Pineapples ripen very rapidly, but will simply not ripen once picked, so be careful when buying them; they should have a full floral scent and the little leaves at the stalk end should come away with ease. Before preparing a pineapple, stand it upside down for about 30 minutes to let the juices redistribute. Cut off the leafy crown, and then cut the fruit crosswise into thick slices. Remove the skin around the edge of the slices and then cut out the woody discs of internal core.

Pineapple is rich in a protein-digesting enzyme called bromelin and is, therefore, used in marinades and to help in the digestion of meat-based meals. Bromelin also curdles milk and cream and will prevent gelatin-based jellies from setting (use agar agar). Pineapple is rich in vitamin C.

## NUTS

### ALMOND *Badaam*

The almond is one of the most important nuts used in cooking worldwide. Related to the peach and the apricot, it is thought to have originated in the Middle East and has certainly been a favorite in Arab sweet and savory cooking for thousands of years. There are two types of almonds: bitter and sweet. The former have more flavor, but are poisonous when raw. The two types are often used together in cooked dishes, as the bitter almonds bring out the flavor of their sweet cousins. Almonds are highly nutritious and

particularly rich in folic acid. Increasingly, they are also thought to have considerable cancer-fighting properties.

### CASHEW *Kaju*

These delicious long white nuts with a distinctive texture are related to the mango and pistachio. Native to Brazil, they were brought to Goa by the Portuguese, and India now rivals Brazil as a producer. As the shell of the fresh nut exudes a blistering oil, usually only the dried shelled nuts are offered for sale. Cashews are rich in minerals, particularly zinc.

### COCONUT *Khopra, Narial*

Because of its abundance and versatility, coconut plays an important role in the cooking of most of India, and southern Asia in general. The mature nut is cracked open (do this carefully, as the juice inside can make a refreshing drink), the flesh is separated into chunks, and the skin is removed. The flesh is then usually grated to a pulp, and this may be used as is (sometimes after brief toasting), or frozen for future use. More often than not, it is used to make coconut milk or cream, by soaking it in hot water. The first soaking process produces the thicker "cream" and subsequent soakings give the thinner "milk."

Desiccated (or dried) shredded coconut flesh is popular in baking and candy-making and can also be used to make coconut cream and milk by soaking it as described above. Frozen and canned coconut cream and milk are readily available and make perfectly acceptable substitutes for fresh, although they often contain additives.

Because the fats in coconut are more highly saturated than in almost anything else in the vegetable kingdom, coconut and coconut products should be used in moderation. In this book I have tried to reduce the quantities used considerably. On the other hand, the nut is totally without cholesterol (unlike similarly saturated animal fats), is rich in iodine and iron, and is one of the best sources of medium-chain fats, thought to play a very important role in the metabolizing of fats in general. Indeed, many coconut-based drugs make use of this property.

### PINE NUTS *Chilghozay*

The seeds of many types of pine trees are edible. The best-known in the West come from the Mediterranean stone pine (*Pinus pinea*) and are very similar to the pine nuts used in the cooking of eastern India. The pine cones are gathered in autumn and winter and stored until summer, when they are dried in the sun, then shaken out of their cones. The very oily nuts have a lovely buttery taste and texture, and are best lightly roasted prior to use. Pine nuts contain a broad range of nutrients and are among the richest sources of protein by weight in the vegetable kingdom.

### PISTACHIO *Pista*

These small pale to dark green nuts (the darker the green, the better the flavor), with an evocative slightly resinous flavor, are native to Asia but are also popular in most Middle Eastern and Mediterranean countries. They are widely used in Indian desserts. For cooking, buy shelled and unsalted nuts. Pistachios are said to help purify the blood and promote liver and kidney activity.

## RICE AND FLOURS

### BASMATI RICE

The average southern Indian is said to be able to recognize at least twenty varieties of rice by sight. In this book, however, I have only suggested the use of (polished white) basmati rice—even for my rice pudding. This long-grain rice grown in the Himalayan foothills is aged for about a year and has a wonderful rich aromatic flavor and fine texture. It also has the advantage of cooking in just over 10 minutes, although it benefits from lengthy rinsing—in a sieve under running water or in several bowls of clean water —and/or soaking prior to cooking. As it tends to elongate during cooking (rather than plump up) and contains less starch than other long-grain varieties, it also produces nice separate grains. More than anything, however, I just love it for its flavor! Despite what some people would have you believe, white rice also retains quite a substantial proportion of the grain's nutrients, particularly its proteins.

### CHAPATI FLOUR

Also known as *ata*, this finely ground whole-wheat flour is found at Indian and Pakistani grocery stores. It is used to make chapatis, parathas and pooris. Finely sifted ordinary whole-wheat flour can also be used for Indian breads.

GRAM FLOUR

Also known as *besan* or *besun*, this fine flour is made from chana dhal (see page 23). It is used to make pakoras and also as a binding agent and to make batters for coating fried food. A combination of gram flour and ordinary whole-wheat flour makes a delicious type of Indian bread called *besun ki roti.*

## DAIRY PRODUCTS

GHEE

This clarified butter is the principal cooking medium of India. For health reasons I have eliminated it from the recipes in this book (except for a little in the Naan recipe on page 124), and replaced it with olive oil or corn oil, as these are both much lower in saturated fats. Because of all the other strong flavors in the food, I think the difference will only possibly be noticed in the bread recipes, where the unctuousness and flavor of ghee is integral.

PANIR

This is fresh curd cheese, usually made at home, used in many ways all over India and Pakistan. See the recipe on page 140.

YOGURT *Raita*

This soured milk product is used in India in innumerable ways, just like cream in European cuisine. When adding yogurt to curries, to give it a thick creamy texture, I always whip it first with a fork and then add it gradually so that it does not curdle. Yogurt used in marinades helps to tenderize meat.

Always use plain unsweetened yogurt. Fortunately, low-fat yogurt is full of flavor, unlike many low-fat versions of other dairy products.

## MISCELLANEOUS

KEWRA WATER

This clear delicately scented liquid, made from the exquisitely scented flowers of the screwpine tree (*Pandanus odoratissimus*), is used to flavor many sweet dishes and some poultry and rice dishes. It can be found in most Indian and Pakistani shops.

ROSE WATER

Rose water is made from essence of rose petals and is a popular flavoring in Middle Eastern and Indian sweets. It is also used in European baking and can be found in many large supermarkets and specialty food stores.

SILVER LEAF *Varg*

These sheets of edible thinly beaten silver leaf are used to decorate special-occasion dishes for festivals and special family events. They can usually be purchased in better Indian and Pakistani shops.

# Snacks and Appetizers

# SHRIMP AND VEGETABLE KEBABS

*These kebabs are coated with breadcrumbs and may be broiled or lightly fried. They may be served either with a salad as an appetizer or as one of the dishes of the main meal.*

SERVES 4
(MAKES 10-12)

PREPARATION
*about 30 minutes*
COOKING
*about 25 minutes*

Calories per serving *340*
Total fat *7 g (20%)*
Saturated fat *1 g*
Protein *16 g*
Carbohydrate *56 g*
Cholesterol per serving
*88 mg*
Vitamins *A, B group, C, E*
Minerals *Calcium,*
*Potassium, Iron, Zinc,*
*Iodine*

*4½ oz peeled cooked shrimp*
*2 potatoes*
*2 carrots*
*2 oz green beans*
*2 oz petits pois*
*2 oz frozen or canned corn , thawed or drained*
*1 tablespoon lemon juice*
*2 tablespoons crushed dried red chilies*

*1 large garlic clove, crushed*
*1-inch piece ginger, shredded*
*1 tablespoon chopped fresh cilantro, plus more whole leaves for garnish*
*salt*
*2½ cups breadcrumbs*
*2 tablespoons corn oil*

**1**   Coarsely chop the shrimp. Peel the potatoes, then cook them whole in boiling salted water until just tender. Drain and allow to cool slightly, then mash lightly with a fork or potato masher and set aside.

**2**   Peel the carrots and cut into very fine matchsticks about ½ inch long. Cut the green beans into similar lengths.

**3**   In a pan of boiling salted water, blanch the green beans, peas, and corn for 2 minutes. Drain and set aside.

**4**   Place all the vegetables and the shrimp in a large bowl. Using a fork, mix everything together. Add the lemon juice, dried chilies, garlic, ginger, and cilantro with salt to taste.

**5**   Once everything is well blended, break off small balls and mold them into round flat shapes in the palms of your hands (the mixture should be sufficient to make 10-12). Dip these into the breadcrumbs and place on a tray.

**6**   Heat half the oil in a large nonstick frying pan. Carefully drop half the kebabs into the frying pan and press them down with a spatula. Cook over a moderate heat for 1-2 minutes on each side, until golden brown. Remove, drain briefly on paper towels, and place on a warmed serving dish. Keep warm while you cook the remaining kebabs in the remaining oil. Serve garnished with cilantro.

*Previous pages: Shrimp and Vegetable Kebabs with a mixed herb salad and Quick Mint and Cucumber Raita (page 145)*

# POTATO KEBABS WITH MINCED SHRIMP FILLING

*These potato kebabs make a delicious starter, served with Date and Tamarind Chutney (page 144) and a raita. If you wish to broil the kebabs, omit the egg and just lightly brush the kebabs with some oil before broiling them on both sides.*

**4-5 medium potatoes**
**2 tablespoons chopped fresh cilantro leaves**
**1 tablespoon chopped fresh mint**
**1-2 fresh red chilies, chopped**
**salt**

**for the filling:**
**6 oz peeled cooked shrimp**
**8 button mushrooms, diced**

**½ teaspoon ginger pulp (page 17)**
**½ teaspoon garlic pulp (page 17)**
**½ teaspoon chili powder**
**1 tablespoon chopped fresh cilantro**
**1 teaspoon lemon juice**
**salt**
**corn oil, for cooking the kebabs**
**1 large egg, beaten**

SERVES 4
(MAKES 8-10)

PREPARATION
*about 30 minutes,*
*plus cooling*
COOKING
*about 20-25 minutes*

Calories per serving *211*
Total fat *5 g (23%)*
Saturated fat *1 g*
Protein *16 g*
Carbohydrate *26 g*
Cholesterol per serving
*184 mg*
Vitamins *A, B group, C, E*
Minerals *Potassium, Iron,*
*Zinc, Selenium, Iodine*

**1**  Peel the potatoes and cut them into chunks. Boil them in plenty of salted water until tender, then drain and mash.

**2**  While the mashed potatoes are still warm, add to them the cilantro, mint, red chilies, and salt to taste. Leave to cool at room temperature.

**3**  To make the filling, coarsely chop the shrimp. Place in a small heavy-bottomed saucepan. Add the mushrooms, followed by the ginger, garlic, chilli, cilantro, lemon juice, and salt to taste.

**4**  Place over moderate heat and cook for 2-3 minutes, stirring continuously. Once all the liquid has evaporated, remove the pan from the heat and transfer its contents to a plate to cool.

**5**  Mold 8-10 golf-ball-size portions of the mashed potato mixture into flat round shapes in the palm of your hand. Make a dimple in the middle of each one and fill with the shrimp and mushroom filling (about a level teaspoon). Fold the potato over the filling and again flatten into a round shape.

**6**  When all the kebabs are ready, pour about 1 tablespoon corn oil into a nonstick frying pan and place over moderate heat. Dip each of the kebabs in the beaten egg and fry, turning at least twice, for 1 to 2 minutes on each side, until golden brown on both sides.

**7**  When all are ready, serve 2 or 3 per person.

# SHALLOT AND JUMBO SHRIMP APPETIZER WITH HONEY AND SCALLOPS

*Frozen shelled jumbo shrimp are readily available from most good supermarkets. If using fresh, peel off the shells and use a knife to remove the black vein of intestinal tract along their length. If using precooked, add them with the scallops and cook for only a minute or so to heat through.*

*This delicious sweet-and-spicy appetizer can be served on a bed of mixed salad leaves, such as lettuce and endive, plus radish, cilantro, and a few slices of red bell pepper, if you wish, for extra texture.*

SERVES 4

PREPARATION
*about 10-15 minutes*
COOKING
*about 10 minutes*

Calories per serving *107*
Total fat *1 g (6%)*
Saturated fat *1 g*
Protein *12 g*
Carbohydrate *14 g*
Cholesterol per serving
*82 mg*
Vitamins *B₃, B₁₂*
Minerals *Potassium, Zinc, Selenium, Iodine*

**12 fresh or frozen jumbo shrimp, peeled and cooked**
**12 fresh or frozen sea scallops**
**2 tablespoons chili and garlic sauce (page 17)**
**3 tablespoons honey**

**½ teaspoon salt**
**2 shallots, finely chopped**
**1 green chili, finely chopped**
**lime wedges, for serving**

**1**  Peel and devein the fresh shrimp as explained above or, if you are using frozen, allow them to defrost completely. Drain and pat dry with paper towels. Do the same with frozen scallops.

**2**  In a kadahi, wok, or deep frying pan, mix the chili and garlic sauce with the honey, salt, and ⅔ cup water. Bring to a boil.

**3**  Lower the heat to very low and add the shallots and green chili. Cook for a minute or so, then add the prawns and gently stir-fry for 1-2 minutes. Add the scallops and stir-fry for 1-2 minutes more until the scallops are just firm when pressed. Do not overcook! Serve warm with wedges of lime.

*Shallot and Jumbo Shrimp Appetizer with Honey and Scallops*

# CHOHLAY
## *Chickpea Snack*

*This sweet-and-sour treat is one of the most popular snacks all over the Indian subcontinent. It may be eaten at any time of the day and makes an excellent accompaniment to almost any meal. I recommend using canned chickpeas as they have just the right texture for this dish.*

SERVES 4

PREPARATION
*about 20 minutes*
COOKING
*about 10 minutes*

Calories per serving *354*
Total fat *6 g (16%)*
Saturated fat *1 g*
Protein *17 g*
Carbohydrate *61 g*
Cholesterol per serving
*None*
Vitamins *B₁, B₃, B₆,*
*Folate, C, E*
Minerals *Calcium,*
*Potassium, Iron, Zinc*

*4 cups canned chickpeas*
*1 large potato, cubed*
*1 medium onion, diced*
*2 tablespoons tamarind paste*
*1 teaspoon mango powder  (page 10)*
*1 teaspoon garam masala*
*1 teaspoon ground coriander*
*½ teaspoon ground ginger*
*1 teaspoon chili powder*

*2 tablespoons ketchup*
*2 tablespoons sugar*
*salt*
*1 tablespoon chopped fresh mint*
*2 tablespoons chopped fresh cilantro*
*4 cherry tomatoes, sliced*
*3 pearl onions, sliced*
*1 red chili*
*1 green chili*

**1**  Drain the chickpeas well and place them in a large serving bowl.

**2**  Boil the potato and onion until soft but not mushy. Drain and set aside.

**3**  In a large bowl, blend together the tamarind, mango powder, garam masala, ground coriander, ginger, chili powder, ketchup, sugar, salt to taste, and ⅔ cup water. Pour this sweet-and-sour sauce over the chickpeas. Add the potato and onion and mix everything together gently.

**4**  Mix in half the mint and cilantro. Garnish with the remaining mint and cilantro, and the tomatoes and onions. Arrange the chilies crossed on top and serve.

# MASALA SHRIMP AND VEGETABLE SAMOSAS

*These adaptations of traditional samosas substitute phyllo pastry for the usual more stodgy wrapping, and they are baked rather than deep-fried. As well as making an interesting and unusual appetizer, they can be served with drinks or as a snack at any time of the day.*

**12 sheets phyllo pastry**
**2 tablespoons peanut oil**
**6 oz peeled cooked shrimp**
**1 tablespoon tomato purée**
**1 teaspoon garam masala**
**1 teaspoon chili powder**
**½ teaspoon ground coriander**
**1 teaspoon garlic pulp (page 17)**
**1 teaspoon ginger pulp (page 17)**

**salt**
**4 tablespoons low-fat fromage blanc**
**1 tablespoon chopped fresh cilantro leaves**
**2 teaspoons lemon juice**
**4 mushrooms, thinly sliced**
**½ red bell pepper, seeded and diced**
**1 carrot, diced**
**2 oz frozen corn kernels, thawed**

SERVES 4
(MAKES 8)

PREPARATION
*about 15 minutes*
COOKING
*15-20 minutes*

Calories per samosa *36*
Total fat *1 g (21%)*
Saturated fat *less than 1 g*
Protein *3 g*
Carbohydrate *5 g*
Cholesterol per serving
*21 mg*
Vitamins *A, B₁₂*
Minerals *Iodine, Selenium, Potassium*

**1** Preheat the oven to 375°F. Keep the sheets of pastry rolled together under a damp cloth as otherwise they dry out fast and become difficult to work. Rinse the shrimp and pat dry with paper towels.

**2** In a small bowl, mix together the tomato purée, garam masala, chili powder, ground coriander, garlic, ginger, salt, fromage blanc, cilantro, lemon juice, and 4 tablespoons water.

**3** Transfer this mixture to a kadahi, wok, or deep frying pan and cook over moderate heat for 1 minute until aromatic.

**4** Add the shrimp, sliced mushrooms, bell pepper, carrot, and corn. Stir-fry over medium to low heat for 5-7 minutes, until the mixture is fairly dry. Remove the mixture from the heat.

**5** Working quickly with 2 or 3 sheets of pastry at a time and using a plate or saucer as a template, cut 2 or 3 rounds about 5 inches in diameter from each sheet. Oil each round lightly and arrange 3 rounds on top of each other. Put about one-eighth of the shrimp and vegetable mixture just to one side of the center of the pastry round and fold the pastry over to make a semicircle. Press down lightly and seal by folding the edges 2 or 3 times like a hem and pinching. Brush the outside of the package lightly with oil.

**6** Once all the samosas are made, put them in the oven and bake for about 25 minutes until just nicely golden.

# MASALA-GRILLED COD STEAKS WITH TOMATO

*These spicy cod steaks make a very attractive appetizer. They can also be served as one of several main-course dishes.*

SERVES 4

PREPARATION
*about 25 minutes,
plus 30 minutes
marinating*
COOKING
*8-12 minutes*

Calories per serving *180*
Total fat *4 g (21%)*
Saturated fat *1 g*
Protein *25 g*
Carbohydrate *11 g*
Cholesterol per serving
*58 mg*
Vitamins *A, B group, C, E*
Minerals *Iron, Selenium,
Iodine, Potassium*

*4 cod steaks, each about 4½ oz*
*1 tablespoon sunflower oil*
*3 tablespoons lemon juice*
*1 teaspoon garlic pulp (page 17)*
*1 teaspoon crushed dried red chilies*
*1 tablespoon chopped fresh cilantro leaves,
plus 4 sprigs for garnish*
*1 large fresh red chili, finely chopped*
*salt*
*2 firm tomatoes, chopped*

*1 teaspoon shredded ginger*
*1 lime, quartered, for serving*

*for the mixed salad:*
*3 leaves iceberg lettuce, torn into strips*
*8-10 whole baby spinach leaves*
*1 red onion, sliced into rings*
*½ cucumber, thinly sliced*
*2 carrots, finely grated*
*1 tablespoon lemon juice*

**1**  Rinse the cod steaks and pat them dry. Place in a heatproof dish.

**2**  In a bowl, mix the oil, lemon juice, garlic, crushed chilies, cilantro, fresh chili and salt to taste. Using a pastry brush, spread the mixture over the cod steaks and set aside for about half an hour.

**3**  When ready to cook, preheat the broiler until it is as hot as you can get it, then turn it down to moderate if you can. Cook the cod steaks for 5-10 minutes, until cooked through (the flesh flakes readily when pushed with a fork). Remove the steaks from the broiler and baste with any juices that have formed around the fish.

**4**  Sprinkle the tomato and shredded ginger over the steaks. Return to the broiler and cook for an additional 1-2 minutes, until the tomatoes have browned lightly.

**5**  When the fish is almost ready, combine the lettuce and spinach leaves, onion, cucumber, and carrot in a large bowl.

**6**  Remove the fish from the broiler, arrange on 4 individual plates and garnish with the cilantro sprigs. Arrange the salad beside the cod steaks and sprinkle with lemon juice and, if you wish, a little salt. Serve with a lime quarter on each plate.

*Masala-grilled Cod Steaks with Tomato*

# AVOCADO WITH SPICY LEMON SHRIMP

*Though avocado is not an Indian fruit, it is one of my favorites.*

SERVES 4

PREPARATION
*about 20 minutes*

Calories per serving *243*
Total fat *22 g (80%)*
Saturated fat *3 g*
Protein *9 g*
Carbohydrate *3 g*
Cholesterol per serving
*92 mg*
Vitamins *B group, C, E*
Minerals *Potassium, Iron,*
*Zinc, Iodine*

*2 avocados*
*zest and 3 tablespoons juice from 1 lemon*
*4½ oz peeled cooked shrimp*
*5 tablespoons low-fat mayonnaise*
*1 teaspoon crushed coriander seeds*
*1 teaspoon crushed dried red chilies*
*2 tablespoons chopped fresh cilantro leaves*

*1 fresh green chili, chopped*
*1 fresh red chili, chopped*

*for the garnish:*
*1 tablespoon sesame seeds*
*4 sprigs fresh cilantro*

1   Halve the avocados and remove the pits. Brush the exposed flesh with a little of the lemon juice to prevent discoloration. Place the avocados, cut side down, on serving plates.

2   Squeeze out any excess water from the shrimp.

3   Mix together the mayonnaise, lemon zest and juice, coriander seeds, dried chilies, cilantro, and fresh green and red chilies. Add the shrimp and blend everything together.

4   Turn the avocado halves cut side up and spoon equal amounts of the filling into each one. Serve garnished with the sesame seeds and fresh cilantro.

# TROUT-FILLED BEEFSTEAK TOMATOES

SERVES 4

PREPARATION
*about 20 minutes*
COOKING
*25-30 minutes*

Calories per serving *182*
Total fat *9 g (44%)*
Saturated fat *2 g*
Protein *16 g*
Carbohydrate *10 g*
Cholesterol per serving
*55 mg*
Vitamins *A, B group, C, E*
Minerals *Potassium, Iron,*
*Zinc, Selenium, Iodine*

*4 large beefsteak tomatoes*
*3 small trout fillets*
*2 tablespoons olive oil*
*1 onion, thinly sliced*
*large pinch onion seeds*
*4 curry leaves*

*2 garlic cloves, halved lengthwise*
*1 teaspoon shredded ginger*
*2 oz shelled peas*
*1 tablespoon chopped fresh cilantro leaves*
*2 fresh red chilies, sliced*
*salt*

1   Cut the tops off the tomatoes and, using a grapefruit knife, remove the flesh (use for a sauce or another dish). Cut the trout fillets into small bite-sized pieces. Preheat a broiler to medium.

2   Heat the olive oil in a kadahi, wok, or deep frying pan and fry the onion, onion seeds, curry leaves, garlic, and ginger for about 30 seconds.

3   Drop in the trout and stir-fry for about 5 minutes until firm, trying not to break up the pieces.

4   Add the peas and cilantro. Cook for 3-5 minutes more. Mix in the chilies and season with salt. Divide the stuffing among the 4 tomatoes.

5   Place the tomatoes on the broiler and cook for about 10-15 minutes, until they begin to brown.

# CHICKEN LIVERS WITH SCALLIONS

*Chicken livers are becoming increasingly popular in India and Pakistan, probably because they are so tasty and economical. Serve them with a salad or on a bed of greens, accompanied by naan (page 124).*

**1 lb chicken livers**
**½ teaspoon turmeric**
**½ teaspoon salt**
**2 tablespoons corn oil**
**3 whole garlic cloves**
**1 teaspoon shredded ginger**

**6 curry leaves**
**2 fresh green chilies, sliced lengthwise**
**small bunch of scallions, thickly sliced at an angle**
**1 teaspoon lemon juice**
**1 tablespoon chopped fresh cilantro**

SERVES 4

PREPARATION
*about 25 minutes*
COOKING
*about 10 minutes*

Calories per serving *162*
Total fat *8 g (46%)*
Saturated fat *2 g*
Protein *21 g*
Carbohydrate *1 g*
Cholesterol per serving *428 mg*
Vitamins *A, B group, C, E*
Minerals *Potassium, Iron, Zinc*

**1** Trim the chicken livers well, removing any fatty tubes or any darkened or discolored edges. Rub the livers with a mixture of the turmeric and salt and then rinse to remove any lingering odors. Set the livers aside on paper towels to drain.

**2** Heat the oil in a kadahi, wok, or deep frying pan over moderate heat. Add the garlic, ginger, and curry leaves, and stir-fry for about 30 seconds.

**3** Add the chicken livers, followed by the fresh chilies and salt to taste, and stir-fry for 5-7 minutes until the livers are firm and lightly browned. Add the scallions and sprinkle in the lemon juice, followed by the fresh cilantro. Cook for about a minute more.

**4** Transfer to a warmed serving dish and serve immediately.

# BROILED CHICKEN BOTI KEBABS

Boti *simply means "pieces of meat." These kebabs go well with the Tomato and Onion Raita on page 142. Served with naan, they can also make a good light lunch. To give a sweet-and-sour flavor to the marinade, omit the mint sauce and garam masala and replace with 2 tablespoons tamarind paste and 3 tablespoons each ketchup and honey.*

SERVES 4

PREPARATION
*about 25 minutes,
plus 30 minutes
marinating*
COOKING
*about 10 minutes*

Calories per serving *164*
Total fat *5 g (25%)*
Saturated fat *1 g*
Protein *21 g*
Carbohydrate *11 g*
Cholesterol per serving
*50 mg*
Vitamins *A, B group, C, E*
Minerals *Calcium,
Potassium, Iron, Zinc,
Iodine*

**10 oz boned skinless chicken**
**¾ cup low-fat plain yogurt**
**1 teaspoon garam masala**
**1 teaspoon ground coriander**
**1 teaspoon ginger pulp (page 17)**
**1 teaspoon mint sauce**
**2 garlic cloves, finely chopped**
**½ teaspoon chili powder**
**1 tablespoon chopped fresh cilantro leaves**
**2 fresh red chilies, chopped**

**1 teaspoon salt**
**8-10 whole shallots**
**1 zucchini, thickly sliced**
**8-10 cherry tomatoes**
**1 large bell green pepper, seeded and cut into chunks**
**1 tablespoon corn oil**
**1 tablespoon lemon juice**
**1 onion, halved and thinly sliced, for garnish**
**few spinach or lettuce leaves, shredded, for garnish**

**1** Cut the chicken into bite-sized cubes and put in a deep bowl.

**2** Put the yogurt in a food processor and add the garam masala, coriander, ginger, mint sauce, garlic, chili powder, cilantro, and 1 chopped red chili, with salt to taste. Process for about 30 seconds. Pour over the chicken, mix well, and leave to marinate for about half an hour. Prepare the vegetables and stir them into the marinade as they are ready.

**3** Preheat a broiler to medium. Add the oil to the marinade and mix everything together well.

**4** Arrange the chicken cubes and vegetables on skewers and broil for 5-10 minutes, turning and brushing with the marinade, until the chicken is cooked through and scorch marks begin to appear on top of the chicken and vegetables.

**5** Serve sprinkled with the lemon juice and garnished with the onion, shredded leaves, and chili.

*Broiled Chicken Boti Kebabs served with Naan (page 124)*

# MUSHROOM AND FRESH CILANTRO SOUP

SERVES 4

PREPARATION
*15-20 minutes*
COOKING
*about 20-25 minutes*

Calories per serving *125*
Total fat *7 g (53%)*
Saturated fat *2 g*
Protein *7 g*
Carbohydrate *8 g*
Cholesterol per serving
*9 mg*
Vitamins *B group, C, E*
Minerals *Calcium,*
*Potassium, Zinc, Iodine,*
*Selenium*

*1 small onion*
*12 oz button mushrooms*
*2 tablespoons olive oil*
*1 whole bay leaf*
*½ teaspoon coarsely ground pepper*
*¼ cup ground almonds*
*¼ teaspoon freshly grated nutmeg*

*salt*
*1¾ cups low-fat milk*
*1 tablespoon chopped fresh cilantro leaves, plus more for garnish*
*1 tablespoon low-fat fromage blanc*
*paprika, for garnish*

1   Dice the onion and wipe the mushrooms clean with a damp cloth; slice both coarsely.
2   Heat the oil in a heavy-bottomed saucepan. Add the onion and bay leaf and cook for 1½ minutes. Add the mushrooms and cook, stirring, for 3-5 minutes until softened.
3   Lower heat slightly and add the pepper, almonds, nutmeg, and salt to taste. Stir in 1¼ cups water and the milk. Heat to just below a boil, cover, and simmer gently for 10 minutes, stirring occasionally.
4   Add the cilantro, carefully transfer the soup to a blender or food processor (in batches if necessary), and process until smooth.
5   Reheat the soup in the pan, stir in the fromage blanc, and serve, garnished with more cilantro and a sprinkling of paprika.

# LEEK AND POTATO SOUP WITH CILANTRO

SERVES 4

PREPARATION
*about 25 minutes*
COOKING
*about 30 minutes*

Calories per serving *421*
Total fat *27 g (58%)*
Saturated fat *14 g*
Protein *12 g*
Carbohydrate *34 g*
Cholesterol per serving
*21 mg*
Vitamins *A, B group, C, E*
Minerals *Calcium,*
*Potassium, Iron, Zinc,*
*Iodine*

*3 leeks, trimmed and coarsely chopped*
*3 medium potatoes, coarsely diced*
*1 celery stalk, trimmed and coarsely chopped*
*1 medium carrot, coarsely chopped*
*2 tablespoons corn oil*
*2½ cups low-fat milk*
*½ teaspoon garlic pulp (page 17)*

*½ teaspoon garam masala*
*salt*
*⅔ cup low-fat sour cream*
*¾ cup low-fat fromage blanc*
*2 tablespoons chopped fresh cilantro leaves, for garnish*

1   In a heavy-bottomed saucepan over moderate heat, fry all the vegetables in the oil, stirring occasionally, for 3-5 minutes.
2   Add 2½ cups water, the milk, garlic, garam masala, and salt to taste. Bring to a boil and simmer until half the liquid has evaporated, 15-20 minutes.
3   Remove from the heat, allow to cool slightly, and stir in the sour cream and fromage blanc. Carefully transfer the soup to a blender or food processor and purée (in batches if necessary). Adjust the seasoning.
4   Return the soup to the pan and heat to just below a boil. Serve garnished with the cilantro.

*Mushroom and Fresh Cilantro Soup served with Naan (page 124)*

# Fish and Shellfish

# FISH FILLETS WITH FENUGREEK SAUCE

*Fenugreek, fresh and dried (I use both in this dish), has a beautiful fragrance. Serve these fillets with Aromatic Rice with Peas (page 126) or plain boiled rice.*

SERVES 4

PREPARATION
*10 minutes*
COOKING
*about 20 minutes*

Calories per serving *141*
Total fat *5 g (33%)*
Saturated fat *2 g*
Protein *23 g*
Carbohydrate *None*
Cholesterol per serving
*63 mg*
Vitamins *B group*
Minerals *Selenium, Iodine, Potassium*

*4 large skinless sole or flounder fillets*
*2 tablespoons low-fat sour cream*
*¼ teaspoon turmeric*
*1 teaspoon garlic pulp (page 17)*
*1 teaspoon crushed dried red chilies*
*large pinch ground fenugreek*
*1 teaspoon ground coriander*

*salt*
*2 tablespoons olive oil*
*large pinch mustard seeds*
*6 curry leaves*
*1 tablespoon fresh fenugreek leaves*
*6-8 cherry tomatoes, for garnish*
*1 fresh green chili, halved lengthwise, for garnish*

**1** Preheat the oven to 375°F. Wash the fish fillets, pat dry, and place in a heatproof dish.

**2** Pour the sour cream into a mixing bowl and add the turmeric, garlic, dried chilies, ground fenugreek, ground coriander, salt to taste, and 1¼ cups water. Whisk everything together well.

**3** Heat the olive oil over medium heat. Add the mustard seeds and curry leaves, wait for about 20 seconds, then remove the pan from the heat.

**4** Add the sour cream sauce to the pan. Using a whisk, mix it in fully and return to the heat. Cook over low heat for about 4 minutes.

**5** Add the fenugreek leaves, then pour the sauce over the fillets. Place the fillets in the oven and cook for 7-10 minutes, until the flesh flakes when pushed with a fork.

**6** Garnish with the cherry tomatoes and the green chili strips to serve.

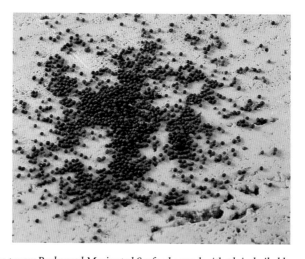

*Previous pages: Barbecued Marinated Seafood served with plain boiled basmati rice*

# LEMON AND GARLIC FISH

*This aromatic dish, lightly flavored with lemon and garlic, goes well with Rice with Pine Nuts (page 128).*

*4 large skinless sole or flounder fillets*
*2 tablespoons olive oil*
*3 scallions, finely chopped*
*1 fresh green chili, seeded and diced*
*1 fresh red chili, seeded and diced*

*2 tablespoons chopped fresh cilantro leaves*
*2 garlic cloves, crushed*
*3 tablespoons lemon juice*
*pinch salt*

1   Rinse the fillets, pat dry, and put in a heatproof dish.

2   In a bowl, mix the oil, scallions, chilies, cilantro, and garlic. Add the lemon juice and salt and set aside.

3   Preheat the broiler. Pour the dressing over the fish and broil for 10-15 minutes, until the flesh flakes when pushed with a fork, turning halfway through and basting from time to time.

SERVES 4

PREPARATION
*about 20 minutes*
COOKING
*10-15 minutes*

Calories per serving *190*
Total fat *8 g (37%)*
Saturated fat *1 g*
Protein *29 g*
Carbohydrate *1 g*
Cholesterol per serving
*79 mg*
Vitamins *B group, C*
Minerals *Selenium, Iodine, Potassium*

# BARBECUED MARINATED SEAFOOD

*I have selected some of my favorite seafood for this dish, but you could choose different fish. It is always better to marinate the pieces to be barbecued overnight for fuller flavors. Serve with rice (see page 46).*

*15 peeled cooked jumbo shrimp*
*2-3 skinless flounder or sole fillets*
*2-3 skinless cod fillets*
*3 skinless trout fillets*
*sliced red onion and cilantro sprigs, for garnish*
*lime or lemon slices, for serving*

*for the marinade :*
*2 tablespoons tomato purée*
*½ cup low-fat plain yogurt*

*1 teaspoon ginger pulp (page 17)*
*1 teaspoon garlic pulp (page 17)*
*1 teaspoon chili powder*
*½ teaspoon turmeric*
*1½ teaspoons ground coriander*
*1 teaspoon ground cumin*
*1 tablespoon chopped fresh cilantro leaves*
*1 tablespoon corn oil*
*2 tablespoons lemon juice*
*salt*

1   To make the marinade, in a large bowl, blend together all of the ingredients with salt to taste.

2   Rinse the shrimp and fish and pat dry. Cut the fish into bite-sized cubes. Place the pieces of fish and the shrimp in the marinade, mix well, and leave in the refrigerator, covered, either overnight or for at least 3 hours, stirring from time to time.

3   Prepare the barbecue well ahead to get it really hot. When ready to cook, remove the fish from the marinade and start to barbecue the pieces of fish and the shrimp a few at a time, getting them nice and brown on both sides. Eat them as they come off the barbecue, accompanied by slices of lime or lemon and garnished with red onion and cilantro.

SERVES 4

PREPARATION
*20 minutes, plus at least 3 hours marinating*
COOKING
*15-20 minutes*

Calories per serving *295*
Total fat *8 g (25%)*
Saturated fat *1 g*
Protein *51 g*
Carbohydrate *5 g*
Cholesterol per serving
*245 mg*
Vitamins *A, B group, E*
Minerals *Calcium, Potassium, Iron, Zinc, Selenium, Iodine*

# COD WITH MUSHROOMS AND GREEN CHILIES

*Green chilies are lightly fried in oil, drained, and added to the cod at the end to give this dish a beautiful aroma and flavor. Serve with freshly cooked chapatis (page 124).*

SERVES 4

PREPARATION
*about 20 minutes*
COOKING
*10-15 minutes*

Calories per serving *149*
Total fat *8 g (25%)*
Saturated fat *1 g*
Protein *14 g*
Carbohydrate *7 g*
Cholesterol per serving
*27 mg*
Vitamins *B group, C, E*
Minerals *Potassium,*
*Selenium, Iodine*

*10 oz skinless cod, coarsely cubed*
*2 tablespoons corn oil*
*5 green chilies, slit down one side and seeded*
*6 curry leaves*
*large pinch onion seeds*
*large pinch mustard seeds*
*2 onions, sliced*
*1 teaspoon ginger pulp (page 17)*

*1 teaspoon garlic pulp (page 17)*
*1 teaspoon chili powder*
*salt*
*1 tablespoon lemon juice*
*4 oz mushrooms, sliced*
*1 tablespoon chopped fresh cilantro leaves, plus more whole leaves, for garnish*

**1**  Rinse the cod, pat dry, and set aside in the refrigerator so the pieces stay firm.

**2**  Heat the corn oil in a deep frying pan. Add the green chilies and fry for about 1 minute. Remove from the pan, draining off as much oil as possible, then drain again on paper towels.

**3**  Add the pieces of cod and stir-fry over moderate heat for about 1½ minutes. Carefully remove from the pan and keep warm.

**4**  In the remaining oil, over moderate heat, fry the curry leaves, onion and mustard seeds, and sliced onions for 2-3 minutes until aromatic and the onions are softened, stirring occasionally.

**5**  Add the ginger, garlic, chili powder, salt, and lemon juice, followed by the mushrooms, and mix well. Return the cod and the fried green chilies to the pan, followed by the cilantro. Mix again gently. Lower the heat, cover the pan, and cook gently for about 6 minutes, checking occasionally to make sure nothing is sticking to the pan.

**6**  Serve garnished with whole cilantro leaves.

*Cod with Mushrooms and Green Chilies*

# FISH FILLETS WITH CREAMY CILANTRO TOPPING

*Serve this dish with a salad of red onion, arugula, and basil, or Cauliflower with Peppers (page 117).*

SERVES 4

PREPARATION
*10 minutes*
COOKING
*about 10 minutes*

Calories per serving *200*
Total fat *7 g (31%)*
Saturated fat *1 g*
Protein *33 g*
Carbohydrate *1 g*
Cholesterol per serving
*92 mg*
Vitamins *B group*
Minerals *Potassium, Zinc, Selenium, Iodine*

**4 large skinless sole or flounder fillets**
**3 tablespoons low-fat fromage blanc**
**1 fresh green chili, chopped**
**2 tablespoons chopped fresh cilantro leaves**
**2 tablespoons lime juice**

**large pinch salt**
**1 teaspoon sesame seeds**
**1 tablespoon corn oil**
**1 fresh red chili, chopped, for garnish**
**lime wedges, for serving**

**1**  Rinse the fillets, pat dry, and put in a heatproof dish.

**2**  Combine the fromage blanc, chili, cilantro, lime juice, and salt, and whisk well. Add the sesame seeds and corn oil to the creamy sauce.

**3**  Preheat the broiler. Using a pastry brush, brush the sauce over the fillets and place them under the broiler for 7-10 minutes, or until they are cooked completely, turning once halfway through. Serve with lime wedges and garnished with chopped red

# COD FILLETS WITH SPICY CHANA DHAL FLOUR COATING

*This spicy fish dish is fairly quick to make and is good served with a dhal and rice.*

SERVES 4

PREPARATION
*about 15 minutes*
COOKING
*about 10 minutes*

Calories per serving *241*
Total fat *7 g (28 %)*
Saturated fat *1 g*
Protein *36 g*
Carbohydrate *9 g*
Cholesterol per serving
*78 mg*
Vitamins *A, B group, C, E*
Minerals *Potassium, Iron, Selenium, Iodine*

**4 large skinless cod fillets**
**2 tablespoons gram flour (page 29)**
**1 tablespoon all-purpose flour**
**1 tablespoon mango powder (page 10)**
**1 teaspoon chili powder**
**1 teaspoon ground ginger**

**1 teaspoon garlic powder**
**pinch salt**
**2 teaspoons crushed coriander seeds**
**2 tablespoons corn oil**
**lemon wedges, for serving**

**1**  Rinse the cod fillets, pat dry, and set aside in the refrigerator to firm up.

**2**  Mix together the gram and all-purpose flours, mango powder, chili powder, ginger, garlic powder, salt, and the crushed coriander seeds.

**3**  Remove the fillets from the refrigerator, dust them with the flour mixture, and set aside.

**4**  Heat half the oil in a large nonstick frying pan. Place 2 of the fillets in the oil, reduce the heat, and cook for 2-3 minutes each side, turning twice to ensure even cooking, until cooked through.

**5**  Transfer the cooked fillets to a warmed platter and cook the remaining fillets in the same way. Serve with lemon wedges as soon as all are cooked.

*Fish Fillets with Creamy Cilantro Topping*

# MONKFISH WITH GARLIC

*Monkfish is a good fish to use for stir-frying as it does not break up easily. This dish, which includes carrots and parsnips, is delicious served with chapatis and a wet dish like a dhal.*

SERVES 4

PREPARATION
*about 20 minutes*
COOKING
*20-25 minutes*

Calories per serving *191*
Total fat *7 g (34%)*
Saturated fat *1 g*
Protein *14 g*
Carbohydrate *19 g*
Cholesterol per serving
*10 mg*
Vitamins *A, B group, C, E*
Minerals *Potassium, Iron,*
*Selenium, Iodine*

**10 oz monkfish fillets**
**2 tablespoons olive oil**
**1 bay leaf**
**3 garlic cloves**
**1 large leek, sliced**
**6 black peppercorns, crushed**
**1 teaspoon crushed dried red chilies**

**large pinch salt**
**2 carrots, cut into matchsticks**
**2 parsnips, cut into matchsticks**
**1 tablespoon chopped fresh mint**
**1 tablespoon chopped fresh cilantro leaves**
**2 fresh red chilies, sliced**
**more whole mint and cilantro leaves, for garnish**

**1** Cut the monkfish it into cubes, then set aside.

**2** Heat the olive oil over moderate heat in a kadahi, wok, or deep frying pan. Add the bay leaf, garlic, leek, peppercorns, and dried chilies. Cook for 2-3 minutes until aromatic, stirring occasionally.

**3** Add the salt, followed by the carrots and parsnips. Cook over low heat for an additional 2-3 minutes, stirring occasionally. Remove from the heat, add the monkfish, and mix it in well before returning the pan to the heat and continuing to stir-fry for about 6 minutes.

**4** Add the mint, cilantro, and sliced fresh chilies. Cover and cook on the lowest possible heat for about 6 minutes more.

**5** Serve immediately, garnished with whole mint and cilantro leaves.

# TROUT WITH NEW POTATOES AND CAULIFLOWER

*Potatoes and cauliflower complement each other beautifully and are both extremely versatile, as much at home with fish and seafood as with meat and poultry. Serve this dish with chapatis.*

SERVES 4

PREPARATION
*about 25 minutes*
COOKING
*20-25 minutes*

Calories per serving *238*
Total fat *9 g (34%)*
Saturated fat *1 g*
Protein *18 g*
Carbohydrate *23 g*
Cholesterol per serving
*None*
Vitamins *B group, C, E*
Minerals *Potassium, Iron,*
*Zinc, Selenium*

**10 oz skinless trout fillets**
**8-10 new potatoes**
**salt**
**2 tablespoons corn oil**
**2 medium onions, sliced**
**¼ teaspoon mixed onion and mustard seeds**
**6 curry leaves**

**½ small cauliflower, separated into florets**
**3 garlic cloves**
**½ teaspoon ginger pulp (page 17)**
**1 teaspoon crushed dried red chilies**
**2 fresh green chilies, sliced**
**1 tablespoon chopped fresh cilantro leaves**
**1 tablespoon lemon juice**

**1** Cut the trout fillets across the grain into thick slices and set aside.

**2** Scrub the potatoes lightly, then halve them. Boil them in salted water for about 15 minutes or until just tender. Drain well.

3  Heat the oil in a kadahi, wok, or deep frying pan. Add the onions, the mixed seeds, and the curry leaves, and fry for about 2 minutes until aromatic and the onions are softened.

4  Add the cauliflower florets, potatoes, garlic cloves, ginger, dried red chilies, and trout. Stir-fry for about 2 minutes, stirring gently to avoid breaking up any of the ingredients.

5  Add the fresh green chilies, cilantro, and lemon juice. Cover and cook over low heat for 1 minute before serving.

# BAKED TROUT WITH SPICY ALMOND AND COCONUT SAUCE

*I am pleased to say that good-quality trout is widely available, making this rich variation on a classic European dish very quick indeed. Serve it with a simple rice dish.*

**2 large whole trout, cleaned**
**2 tablespoons lemon juice**
**2 tablespoons tomato purée**
**1 tablespoon ground almonds**
**1 teaspoon ginger pulp (page 17)**
**1 teaspoon Tabasco sauce**
**1 teaspoon garlic pulp (page 17)**
**1 teaspoon garam masala**
**3 tablespoons low-fat plain yogurt**
**salt**
**½ cup coconut milk**

**1 tablespoon chopped fresh cilantro leaves**
**2 tablespoons corn oil**
**1 small bay leaf**
**2 black cardamom pods**
**1½-inch piece cinnamon stick**

**for the garnish:**
**sliced almonds**
**lemon wedges**
**fresh bay leaves**

SERVES 4

PREPARATION
*about 15 minutes*
COOKING
*15-20 minutes*

Calories per serving *207*
Total fat *12 g (54%)*
Saturated fat *2 g*
Protein *18 g*
Carbohydrate *6 g*
Cholesterol per serving
*54 mg*
Vitamins *B group, C, E*
Minerals *Potassium, Iron, Selenium, Iodine*

1  Rinse the trout under running water and pat dry with paper towels. Sprinkle the fish with half the lemon juice and place them in an ovenproof dish just big enough to hold them in a single layer.

2  Preheat the oven to 375°F. In a bowl, mix together the tomato purée, ground almonds, ginger, Tabasco sauce, garlic, garam masala, yogurt, salt, coconut milk, fresh cilantro, and the remaining lemon juice. Pour in ½ cup water and blend everything together.

3  In a frying pan, heat the oil with the bay leaf, cardamom pods and cinnamon for about 30 seconds. Pour in the sauce and bring to a boil. Reduce the heat and cook for an additional 1-2 minutes. Pour the sauce over the trout.

4  Bake for 10-15 minutes, until cooked through (the flesh flakes readily when pushed with the tip of a knife).

5  Serve the fish with the garnish.

*Overleaf left to right: Monkfish with Garlic, Baked Trout with Spicy Almond and Coconut Sauce*

# JUMBO SHRIMP DOPIAZA WITH MANGO POWDER

SERVES 4

*Dopiaza simply means "double onions," indicating a recipe that calls for masses of them. Mango powder gives this dish a delicious sour tone. Serve with plain boiled rice.*

PREPARATION
*about 15 minutes*
COOKING
*20-25 minutes*

Calories per serving *149*
Total fat *6 g (39%)*
Saturated fat *1 g*
Protein *11 g*
Carbohydrate *13 g*
Cholesterol per serving
*105 mg*
Vitamins *B group, C, E*
Minerals *Potassium, Iron,*
*Selenium, Iodine*

**14-16 peeled cooked jumbo shrimp**
**2 tablespoons corn oil**
**4 onions, thinly sliced**
**large pinch onion seeds**
**4 curry leaves**
**1 teaspoon garlic pulp (page 17)**
**1 teaspoon ginger pulp (page 17)**

**1 teaspoon chili powder**
**salt**
**½ teaspoon turmeric**
**2 teaspoons mango powder (page 10)**
**2 fresh green chilies, sliced**
**2 firm tomatoes, quartered**
**1 table spoon chopped fresh cilantro leaves**

**1**　Rinse the shrimp and pat dry with paper towels.
**2**　Heat the oil over moderate heat in a deep frying pan or a heavy-bottomed saucepan. Add the onions and cook, stirring frequently, until golden brown.
**3**　Add the onion seeds and curry leaves, and stir-fry for about 2 minutes until aromatic. Add the garlic, ginger, chili powder, salt, turmeric, and mango powder, and stir-fry for an additional 3 minutes.
**4**　Add the shrimp, chilies, tomatoes, and most of the cilantro. Lower the heat, cover the pan, and cook for 5-7 minutes until the shrimp are just firm. Serve garnished with the remaining cilantro.

# SHRIMP WITH PEAS AND RED PEPPER

SERVES 4

PREPARATION
*about 15 minutes*
COOKING
*15-20 minutes*

Calories per serving *169*
Total fat *7 g (37%)*
Saturated fat *1 g*
Protein *14 g*
Carbohydrate *13 g*
Cholesterol per serving
*123 mg*
Vitamins *A, B group, C, E*
Minerals *Potassium, Iron,*
*Zinc, Selenium, Iodine*

**6 oz peeled cooked shrimp**
**2 tablespoons corn oil**
**2 onions, diced**
**1 bay leaf**
**¼ teaspoon white cumin seeds**
**2 garlic cloves, sliced in half**
**1 teaspoon ginger pulp (page 17)**

**½ teaspoon chili powder**
**½ teaspoon ground coriander**
**salt to taste**
**1¼ cups shelled peas**
**1 large red bell pepper, seeded and coarsely diced**
**1 tablespoon chopped fresh cilantro leaves**
**juice of ½ lemon**

**1**　Rinse the shrimp and pat dry with paper towels.
**2**　In a kadahi, wok, or deep frying pan, heat the oil over moderate heat. Add the onions, bay leaf, and cumin, and fry for 2 minutes until aromatic.
**3**　Add the garlic, ginger, chili powder, coriander, and salt. Stir-fry over medium to low heat for 1 minute. Add the shrimp and stir-fry for 4 minutes.
**4**　Add the peas, red pepper, and cilantro. Cover and cook for about 6 minutes, stirring occasionally.
**5**　Stir in a little lemon juice just before serving.

*Jumbo Shrimp Dopiaza with Mango Powder*

# PASTA WITH SHRIMP AND SUN-DRIED PEPPERS

*Sun-dried bell peppers are becoming easier to find in supermarkets and health-food stores.*

**8 oz small pasta shells or spirals**
**2 tablespoons corn oil**
**15 peeled cooked shrimp**
**2 garlic cloves, finely chopped**
**1 tablespoon shredded ginger**
**4-6 curry leaves**

**2 scallions, finely chopped**
**1 medium zucchini, sliced**
**1 yellow bell pepper, seeded and sliced**
**3 sun-dried bell peppers, cut into large slices**
**3 fresh green chilies, diced**
**1 tablespoon chopped fresh cilantro leaves**

**SERVES 4**

**PREPARATION**
*about 20 minutes*
**COOKING**
*about 20 minutes*

Calories per serving *313*
Total fat *7 g (21%)*
Saturated fat *1 g*
Protein *16 g*
Carbohydrate *49 g*
Cholesterol per serving
*88 mg*
Vitamins *A, B group, C, E*
Minerals *Potassium, Iron, Zinc, Selenium, Iodine*

**1** Boil the pasta according to the package instructions until just tender. Drain and set aside. Stir in a few drops of the oil to prevent the pieces of pasta sticking together.

**2** Rinse the shrimp and pat dry with paper towels.

**3** Heat the corn oil over moderate heat in a kadahi, wok, or deep frying pan. Add the garlic, ginger, and curry leaves. After about 45 seconds, add the chopped scallions, zucchini slices, bell peppers, and sun-dried peppers, and stir-fry for about 3 minutes.

**4** Add the shrimp, followed by the green chilies, cilantro, and cooked pasta. Stir-fry for an additional 2 minutes and serve immediately.

*Pasta with Shrimp and Sun-Dried Peppers*

# BALTI JUMBO SHRIMP WITH MUSHROOMS

*The cuisine of Baltistan, one of the northernmost provinces of Pakistan, is not very well known in America. Traditionally cooked in a* kadahi, *Balti dishes are usually stir-fried and are characterized by their fresh full flavors.*

*Frozen shelled jumbo shrimp are readily available from most good supermarkets. If using fresh, peel off the shells and use a knife to remove the black vein of intestinal tract along their length. You can use smaller peeled cooked shrimp, but add these later with the mushrooms as they require only very brief cooking.*

SERVES 4

PREPARATION
*about 15 minutes*
COOKING
*10-15 minutes*

Calories per serving *138*
Total fat *6 g (42%)*
Saturated fat *1 g*
Protein *13 g*
Carbohydrate *8 g*
Cholesterol per serving
*110 mg*
Vitamins *B group, C, E*
Minerals *Potassium, Iron,
Zinc, Selenium, Iodine*

**8 oz fresh or frozen jumbo shrimp**
**2 cups mushrooms**
**2 tablespoons corn oil**
**2 onions, sliced**
**½ teaspoon fennel seeds**

**1 teaspoon crushed dried red chilies**
**2 garlic cloves, sliced**
**1 green bell pepper, seeded and diced**
**2 tablespoons chopped fresh cilantro leaves**

1  If using fresh shrimp, peel and devein as described above; if using frozen, allow them to defrost completely, drain any excess liquid, and pat dry with paper towels.

2  Wipe the mushrooms with a damp cloth and slice thickly.

3  Heat the oil in a kadahi, wok, or deep frying pan. Add the sliced onions and the fennel seeds and cook over fairly high heat for a few minutes until the onions are soft and golden.

4  Add the dried chilies and garlic, followed by the shrimp. Cook, stirring occasionally, for 5-7 minutes. Add the mushrooms and bell pepper, and cook 2-3 minutes more, stirring occasionally.

5  Sprinkle the cilantro on top to serve.

*Balti Jumbo Shrimp with Mushrooms served with Naan (page 124)*

# Meat and Poultry

# SPICED ROASTED CORNISH HENS

*This recipe also works well with other small poultry, such as guinea hens and quail.*

SERVES 4

PREPARATION
*about 10 minutes*
COOKING
*about 45 minutes*

Calories per serving *241*
Total fat *16 g (60%)*
Saturated fat *4 g*
Protein *17 g*
Carbohydrate *9 g*
Cholesterol per serving
*76 mg*
Vitamins *B group, E*
Minerals *Potassium, Iron,*
*Zinc, Selenium, Iodine*

*2 cornish hens*
*1½ tablespoons corn oil*
*4 shallots, sliced*
*1 teaspoon garlic pulp (page 17)*
*1 teaspoon ginger pulp (page 17)*
*1 teaspoon chili powder*
*1 teaspoon ground cumin*
*1½ teaspoons ground coriander*

*1 tablespoon ground almonds*
*salt*
*¼ teaspoon ground cardamom seeds*
*3 tablespoons low-fat plain yogurt*
*1 red onion, chopped, for garnish*
*1 tomato, chopped, for garnish*
*1 tablespoon chopped fresh green chili, for garnish*

**1**  Preheat the oven to 375°F. Wash and pat dry the cornish hens. Place on a heatproof dish and brush inside and out with the oil.

**2**  Heat the remaining oil in a frying pan. Add the shallots and fry over moderate heat until soft and golden brown.

**3**  In a small bowl, mix together the garlic, ginger, chili powder, cumin, ground coriander, almonds, salt to taste, cardamom, and yogurt. Pour over the onions and quickly stir-fry for about 2 minutes.

**4**  Remove from the heat, transfer the sauce to a food processor, and process for about 30 seconds or until smooth.

**5**  Pour the sauce over the cornish hens and roast in the oven for 30-35 minutes until golden and cooked through, basting occasionally.

**6**  Serve the cornish hens split in half, garnished with red onion, tomato and chili.

*Previous pages: Spiced Roasted Cornish Hen served with a Saffron Rice Mold (page 129), Hara Masala Lamb Kebabs (page 94)*

# BASMATI RICE WITH CHICKEN
# AND VEGETABLES

*Here basmati rice is cooked with a few fragrant whole spices and then added to a delicious mixture of chicken and vegetables. Accompany with the refreshing Quick Mint and Cucumber Raita on page 145 for a complete meal.*

**2 cups basmati rice**
**1 cinnamon stick**
**2 black cardamom pods**
**½ teaspoon mixed colored peppercorns**
**3 tablespoons chopped fresh cilantro leaves**
**salt**
**1 tablespoon olive oil**
**2 tablespoons corn oil**
**1 onion, sliced**
**1½ teaspoons ginger pulp (page 17)**

**1 teaspoon garlic pulp (page 17)**
**1 teaspoon chili powder**
**1½ teaspoons garam masala**
**1 tablespoon ground almonds**
**2 tablespoons coconut milk**
**8 oz skinless boned chicken, cut into strips**
**3 tablespoons lemon juice**
**2 oz shelled peas**
**2 oz corn kernels**
**1 red bell pepper, seeded and sliced**

SERVES 4

PREPARATION
*about 25 minutes*
COOKING
*30-35 minutes*

Calories per serving *422*
Total fat *13 g (27%)*
Saturated fat *2 g*
Protein *20 g*
Carbohydrate *56 g*
Cholesterol per serving
*51 mg*
Vitamins *B group, C, E*
Minerals *Potassium, Iron, Zinc*

**1**  Rinse the rice until the water runs clear.

**2**  Place the rice in a saucepan with the cinnamon, cardamom, peppercorns, and 1 tablespoon of the cilantro. Add 3 cups water, salt to taste, and the olive oil. Bring to a boil over high heat. Lower the heat, stir the rice gently, and cover with a lid. Cook for 15-20 minutes, until the rice is just tender. Remove from the heat and set aside.

**3**  In a large kadahi, wok, or deep frying pan, heat the corn oil. Add the onions and fry over moderate heat until golden brown.

**4**  Reduce the heat and add the ginger, garlic, chili powder, garam masala, ground almonds, coconut milk, and salt to taste. Stir-fry all the ingredients for about 2 minutes until aromatic.

**5**  Add the chicken pieces and cook, stirring occasionally, for about 6 minutes. Add the lemon juice, followed by the peas, corn, and bell pepper. Stir-fry for an additional 2 minutes, then add another tablespoon of cilantro. Add the cooked rice and gently combine.

**6**  Cover with either a lid or foil and cook over very low heat for 3-5 minutes before serving, garnished with the remaining cilantro.

# ROASTED CHICKEN
# WITH SPICY MUSHROOMS

*For roasting, I favor small chickens (no bigger than about 3¼ lbs) as they are usually tastier and are also easier and quicker to cook. Choose the best quality extra-virgin olive oil available for this dish, as it will add extra flavor.*

SERVES 4

PREPARATION
*20 minutes*
COOKING
*35-40 minutes,*
*plus 5 minutes*
*resting*

Calories per serving *515*
Total fat *36 g (63%)*
Saturated fat *9 g*
Protein *45 g*
Carbohydrate *3 g*
Cholesterol per serving
*206 mg*
Vitamins *B group, C, E*
Minerals *Potassium, Iron,*
*Zinc, Selenium, Iodine*

*1 chicken, about 2½-3¼ lbs*
*1 tablespoon extra-virgin olive oil*
*salt*
*½ teaspoon coarsely ground black pepper*

*for the spicy mushrooms:*
*2 tablespoons extra-virgin olive oil*
*1 onion, finely diced*
*1 bay leaf*

*½ teaspoon mixed colored peppercorns*
*1 teaspoon ground coriander*
*1 large pinch freshly ground black pepper*
*large pinch turmeric*
*salt*
*8-10 button mushrooms, sliced*
*2 tablespoons chopped fresh cilantro leaves*
*1 fresh red chili, chopped*
*2 tablespoons low-fat sour cream*

**1**  Preheat the oven to 375°F. Cut the chicken into quarters. Brush the bird all over with olive oil and sprinkle with salt and pepper.

**2**  Place the chicken in a heatproof dish and roast for 35-40 minutes until golden and cooked through, basting once or twice.

**3**  Meanwhile, to make the spicy mushrooms, heat the olive oil over moderate heat for 20-30 seconds. Add the onion, bay leaf, and peppercorns, and fry for about 2 minutes. Remove from the heat and add the ground coriander, black pepper, turmeric, and salt to taste. Return the pan to the heat and fry the spices for an additional 30 seconds.

**4**  Stir in the mushrooms, half of the cilantro, and the red chili, and stir-fry for another minute. Pour in the sour cream, blend it in with all the other ingredients, and warm through for about 1 minute. Remove from the heat.

**5**  Allow the roast chicken to sit in a warm place for about 5 minutes after it comes out of the oven, then cut it into pieces and arrange on a warmed serving dish (add any juices from the bird to the mushrooms). Remove the skin if you want to keep the fat and calorie counts down. Serve with the mushrooms spooned over the top and garnished with the remaining cilantro.

*Roasted Chicken with Spicy Mushrooms*

# HALEEM
## *Cracked Wheat with Strips of Chicken*

*This dish is traditionally made with lamb. The chicken version here is perhaps healthier. It is usually served with ghee, but I suggest using olive oil instead for equally delicious results.*

SERVES 4

PREPARATION
*about 25 minutes,
plus overnight
soaking*
COOKING
*about 30 minutes*

Calories per serving *355*
Total fat *14 g (36%)*
Saturated fat *2 g*
Protein *23 g*
Carbohydrate *36 g*
Cholesterol per serving
*64 mg*
Vitamins *B group, C, E*
Minerals *Calcium,
Potassium, Iron, Zinc,
Selenium, Iodine*

**1 cup cracked wheat (bulghur)**
**10 oz skinless boned chicken**
**3 tablespoons corn oil**
**2 onions, thinly sliced**
**1 cinnamon stick**
**4 black peppercorns**
**2 black cardamom pods**
**1½ teaspoons garam masala**
**1½ teaspoons ginger pulp (page 17)**
**1½ teaspoons garlic pulp (page 17)**
**1 teaspoon ground coriander**

**2 teaspoons chili powder**
**1 cup plain yogurt**
**salt**
**2 tablespoons chopped fresh cilantro leaves**
**2 fresh green chilies, chopped**

**for garnish:**
**1 tablespoon finely shredded fresh ginger**
**1 onion, diced**
**2-3 tablespoons olive oil (optional)**
**whole cilantro sprigs**

**1**  In a large bowl, soak the cracked wheat overnight in plenty of water to cover generously.

**2**  Cut the skinless chicken pieces into strips about ½ inch thick.

**3**  Heat the corn oil in a kadahi, wok, or deep frying pan. Add the onions and whole spices, and fry over low to moderate heat until the onions are golden brown.

**4**  Meanwhile, in a large bowl, mix together the garam masala, ginger, garlic, ground coriander, chili powder, yogurt, and salt to taste. Mix the chicken pieces into the yogurt mixture.

**5**  When the onions are ready, pour the chicken mixture into the onions and stir-fry over moderate heat for a minute or two.

**6**  Partly cover with a lid and let the chicken cook

for 7-10 minutes, stirring occasionally. Remove from the heat and set aside.

**7**  Drain the cracked wheat, place it in a food processor, and grind for 1-1½ minutes, gradually adding 2 cups water to loosen the mixture.

**8**  Return the chicken to the heat and add the cracked wheat. Stir-fry over low to moderate heat for 5-7 minutes, stirring continuously so that it does not stick to the bottom of the pan.

**9**  Add the chopped cilantro and half the green chilies. If you feel the consistency is too thick (it should be like a thick soup), add a little more water. Adjust the seasonings to taste.

**10** Transfer to a warmed serving plate and sprinkle with the remaining chilies, and the other garnishes.

*Cracked Wheat with Strips of Chicken served with Naan (page 124)*

# CHAR-BROILED LEMON CHICKEN

SERVES 4

PREPARATION
*about 20 minutes*
COOKING
*10-15 minutes*

Calories per serving *258*
Total fat *12 g (43%)*
Saturated fat *3 g*
Protein *35 g*
Carbohydrate *2 g*
Cholesterol per serving
*126 mg*
Vitamins *A, B group, C, E*
Minerals *Potassium, Iron,*
*Zinc, Selenium*

*1 chicken, about 2½-3¼ lbs*
*1 tablespoon olive oil*
*1½ teaspoons garlic pulp (page 17)*
*grated zest of 1 and juice of 2 lemons*
*salt*
*1 teaspoon crushed dried red chilies*

*for garnish:*
*bunch of watercress*
*1 lemon, sliced*
*8-10 cherry tomatoes*
*1 tablespoon chopped fresh cilantro leaves*

**1** Preheat the broiler. Quarter the chicken and remove the skin. Using a sharp knife, make small slashes diagonally across the flesh to let flavors and heat penetrate.

**2** In a small bowl, mix together the oil, garlic pulp, the lemon zest and juice, and salt to taste. Brush mixture all over the chicken pieces and then sprinkle with the crushed dried red chilies.

**3** Broil for 10-15 minutes, turning the pieces halfway through. Check with a sharp knife or a skewer to see that the chicken is completely cooked (the juices run clear).

**4** Serve on a bed of watercress, garnished with the lemon slices, tomatoes, and cilantro.

# BROILED CHICKEN KEBABS

SERVES 4

PREPARATION
*15-20 minutes,*
*plus 3 hours*
*marinating*
COOKING
*15-20 minutes*

Calories per serving *308*
Total fat *23 g (67%)*
Saturated fat *7 g*
Protein *22 g*
Carbohydrate *4 g*
Cholesterol per serving
*113 mg*
Vitamins *B group*
Minerals *Potassium, Iron,*
*Zinc, Iodine*

*1 lb skinless boned chicken*
*¾ cup low-fat plain yogurt*
*2 tablespoons lemon juice*
*1½ teaspoons garlic pulp (page 17)*
*1½ teaspoons chili powder*
*1½ teaspoons ginger pulp (page 17)*

*salt*
*2 tablespoons finely chopped fresh cilantro leaves*
*1 tablespoon corn oil*
*plain boiled basmati rice, for serving*
*1 lime, sliced, for garnish*

**1** Cut the chicken into 1½-2-inch cubes. Set aside.

**2** In a large bowl, whisk the yogurt with the lemon juice, garlic, chili powder, ginger, salt to taste, and 1¼ cups water.

**3** Drop the chicken pieces into the yogurt mixture. Add half the cilantro, and mix everything together. Leave to marinate at room temperature for at least 3 hours.

**4** Preheat the broiler. Pick out the chicken pieces, shaking off as much marinade as possible, and place on 4 skewers. Place the skewers on a heat-proof dish and brush with the oil.

**5** Turn the broiler down to moderate. Place the skewers under the broiler and cook for 7-10 minutes until well browned and cooked through, then turn them over to ensure even cooking. Any burn marks that appear will only help to give the chicken a char-grilled flavor.

**6** Served on a bed of boiled rice, garnished with the remaining cilantro and a few lime slices.

# BAKED COCONUT CHICKEN WITH SPICY MASHED PARSNIPS

*These spicy parsnips have an intriguing sweet-and-sour flavor and make a delicious alternative to mashed potatoes as an accompaniment.*

*1 chicken, about 3¼ lbs*
*1½ tablespoons olive oil*
*1 onion, diced*
*1 bay leaf*
*2 cloves*
*1-inch piece cinnamon stick*
*3 garlic cloves, crushed*
*1 teaspoon shredded ginger*
*7 tablespoons coconut milk*
*1 teaspoon chili powder*
*1 teaspoon sugar*
*1 tablespoon lemon juice*
*salt*

*1 tablespoon chopped fresh cilantro leaves*
*1½ tablespoons cashew nuts*
*2 tablespoons golden raisins*

*for the spicy mashed parsnips:*
*2 lbs parsnips, coarsely chopped*
*2 tablespoons olive oil*
*½ red bell pepper, seeded and diced*
*1 fresh green chili, chopped*
*1 teaspoon mango powder (page 10)*
*1 tablespoon chopped fresh cilantro leaves*
*1 tablespoon chopped fresh mint*

SERVES 4

PREPARATION
*about 30 minutes*
COOKING
*40-45 minutes*

Calories per serving *640*
Total fat *29 g (40%)*
Saturated fat *6 g*
Protein *56 g*
Carbohydrate *43 g*
Cholesterol per serving
*201 mg*
Vitamins *B group, C, E*
Minerals *Calcium, Potassium, Iron, Zinc, Selenium, Iodine*

**1**  Preheat the oven to 375°F. Skin the chicken and cut it into about 8 pieces.

**2**  Heat the oil in a kadahi, wok, or deep frying pan over moderate heat. Add the onion, bay leaf, cloves, cinnamon, garlic, ginger, 3 tablespoons of the coconut milk, the chili powder, sugar, lemon juice, ⅔ cup water, and salt to taste. Cook for 2-4 minutes until semi-dry.

**3**  Add the cilantro, cashew nuts, and golden raisins. Stir-fry for about 2 minutes over low heat.

**4**  Add the chicken pieces, followed by the remaining coconut milk. Transfer to an ovenproof dish and cook in the oven for 35-40 minutes, until the chicken is cooked through.

**5**  While the chicken is cooking, make the spicy mashed parsnips. Cook the parsnips in boiling salted water for 15-18 minutes, until tender. Drain well and mash using a potato masher. Place in a bowl and add the olive oil, bell pepper, green chili, mango powder, cilantro, mint, and salt to taste. Blend everything together and serve with the chicken.

# CHICKEN BREASTS WITH MANGO SAUCE

*Try to choose thin chicken breasts for this dish as they need to be broiled fairly quickly. It helps to remove the little "fillet" on the underside of the breast (use these for another purpose, such as a salad, since they cook in seconds). This makes it easier to flatten the breasts.*

SERVES 4

PREPARATION
*about 20 minutes*
COOKING
*about 15 minutes*

Calories per serving *174*
Total fat *11 g (57%)*
Saturated fat *2 g*
Protein *13 g*
Carbohydrate *6 g*
Cholesterol per serving
*35 mg*
Vitamins *A, B group, C, E*
Minerals *Potassium*

**2 skinless boned chicken breasts**
**1 tablespoon olive oil**
**2 tablespoons lemon juice**
**salt**
**1 tablespoon finely chopped fresh cilantro leaves, for garnish**
**1 fresh green chili, finely chopped, for garnish**

**for the mango sauce:**
**2 tablespoons sunflower oil**

**large pinch onion seeds**
**6 curry leaves**
**3 tomatoes, sliced**
**1 teaspoon ginger pulp (page 17)**
**1 teaspoon garlic pulp (page 17)**
**2 tablespoons mango chutney**
**1 teaspoon chili powder**
**salt**
**1 tablespoon chopped fresh cilantro leaves**
**1 tablespoon low-fat sour cream**

**1**   Rinse the chicken breasts and pat them dry. Remove the fillets and flatten the breasts. Using a sharp knife, make 2 diagonal slits on each breast to allow the flavors and heat to penetrate the flesh more easily.

**2**   In a small bowl, mix the olive oil, lemon juice, and a little salt. Using a pastry brush, brush the mixture all over the breasts and chill.

**3**   To make the mango sauce, heat the sunflower oil in a kadahi, wok, or deep frying pan over moderate heat. Add the onion seeds and curry leaves and fry for about 30 seconds until aromatic. Add the sliced tomato and stir-fry for about 2 minutes.

Add the ginger, garlic, mango chutney, chili powder, salt to taste, and cilantro, and stir-fry for about 3 minutes until aromatic. Add the sour cream and remove from the heat. Keep warm.

**4**   Preheat the broiler and broil the chicken breasts for 3-4 minutes on each side, until light golden brown, basting occasionally.

**5**   Serve the chicken breasts on a warmed serving dish, with the sauce poured all around them and garnished with the cilantro and green chilies. If you like, you can cut the breasts across at an angle into slices, then fan the slices out.

*Chicken Breasts with Mango Sauce served with Chapati (page 124)*

# HOT AND SPICY CHICKEN STIR-FRY WITH SESAME

*Make this quick stir-fry to use up any leftover roasted chicken or start from scratch with fresh boned chicken as here. If using cooked chicken, omit step 3 and just add it with the vegetables.*

**6 oz skinless boned chicken**
**2 tablespoons corn oil**
**1 teaspoon garlic pulp (page 17)**
**1 teaspoon ginger pulp (page 17)**
**1 teaspoon chili powder**
**1 teaspoon ground coriander**
**salt**

**1 leek, sliced**
**8-10 button mushrooms, thickly sliced**
**½ green bell pepper, seeded and coarsely chopped**
**½ red bell pepper, seeded and coarsely chopped**
**2 tablespoons chopped fresh cilantro leaves**
**1 tablespoon white sesame seeds**
**1 tablespoon lemon juice**

SERVES 4

PREPARATION
*about 15 minutes*
COOKING
*about 10 minutes*

Calories per serving *113*
Total fat *6 g (48%)*
Saturated fat *1 g*
Protein *13 g*
Carbohydrate *3 g*
Cholesterol per serving
*31 mg*
Vitamins *A, B group, C, E*
Minerals *Potassium, Iron, Zinc*

1  Cut the chicken into bite-sized pieces. Set aside.

2  In a small bowl, combine the oil, garlic, ginger, chili powder, ground coriander, and salt to taste. Pour into a kadahi, wok, or deep frying pan, and stir-fry over moderate heat for about 30 seconds until aromatic.

3  Add the chicken pieces and toss to blend everything together. Continue stir-frying the contents of the pan over moderate heat for about 5 minutes.

4  Add the leek, the mushrooms, green and red bell peppers, and half the cilantro, and stir-fry for an additional 5 minutes.

5  Just before serving, add the sesame seeds and sprinkle with the lemon juice. Serve garnished with the remaining cilantro.

*Hot and Spicy Chicken Stir-Fry with Sesame served with Naan (page 124)*

# ROASTED CHICKEN WITH LIME AND HERBS

SERVES 4

PREPARATION
*about 20 minutes,
plus 1 hour
marinating*
COOKING
*35-40 minutes*

Calories per serving *186*
Total fat *7 g (36%)*
Saturated fat *1 g*
Protein *28 g*
Carbohydrate *2 g*
Cholesterol per serving
*79 mg*
Vitamins *B group, C, E*
Minerals *Potassium, Iron,
Zinc, Iodine*

*4 chicken quarters
2 tablespoons virgin olive oil
1 teaspoon ginger pulp (page 17)
1 teaspoon garlic pulp (page 17)
4 tablespoons lime juice
1 fresh green chili, finely chopped
6 tablespoons chopped fresh cilantro leaves*

*1 tablespoon chopped fresh mint, plus more
shredded leaves for garnish
salt
1 teaspoon freshly ground black pepper
2 tomatoes, sliced
lime wedges, for serving*

1   Remove the skin from the chicken, prick it all over with a fork, and set aside in a heatproof dish.
2   In a small bowl, mix together the oil, ginger, garlic, lime juice, chilies, cilantro, mint, and salt to taste. Mix well and pour over the chicken, then brush with a pastry brush to coat evenly. Sprinkle with the black pepper and top with the sliced tomatoes. Cover and leave to marinate for about 1 hour.
3   Preheat the oven to 375°F. Cook for 35-40 minutes until browned and cooked through, basting once or twice. Serve with lime wedges, garnished with shredded mint.

# HOT ACHAARI CHICKEN

*Achaar means "pickle" and this chicken dish calls for spices that are usually used to make pickles.*

SERVES 4

PREPARATION
*about 20 minutes*
COOKING
*about 15 minutes*

Calories per serving *142*
Total fat *7 g (42%)*
Saturated fat *1 g*
Protein *15 g*
Carbohydrate *7 g*
Cholesterol per serving
*39 mg*
Vitamins *B group*
Minerals *Iron, Selenium,
Potassium*

*8 oz skinless chicken breast fillet
2 tablespoons olive oil
1 heaping teaspoon mixed equal parts cumin
seeds, crushed coriander seeds, mustard seeds,
onion seeds, fennel seeds, and fenugreek seeds
6-8 whole curry leaves
2 onions, finely chopped
1 teaspoon ginger pulp (page 17)
1 teaspoon garlic pulp (page 17)*

*1 teaspoon chili powder
¼ teaspoon turmeric
1 teaspoon ground cumin
1 teaspoon ground coriander
1 tablespoon tomato purée
salt
2 fresh red chilies, chopped
1 tablespoon chopped fresh cilantro leaves*

1   Cut the chicken into cubes and set aside.
2   Heat the olive oil in a kadahi, wok, or deep frying pan. Add the mixed seeds and fry over a moderate heat for 30-40 seconds until aromatic.
3   Add the curry leaves, onions, ginger, garlic, chili powder, turmeric, ground cumin, ground coriander, tomato purée, salt to taste, and ⅔ cup water. Add the chicken and stir-fry for about 3 minutes.
4   Lower the heat, cover the pan, and cook over very low heat for 5-7 minutes, stirring occasionally.
5   Just before serving, stir in the chopped chilies and the cilantro.

*Roasted Chicken with Lime and Herbs*

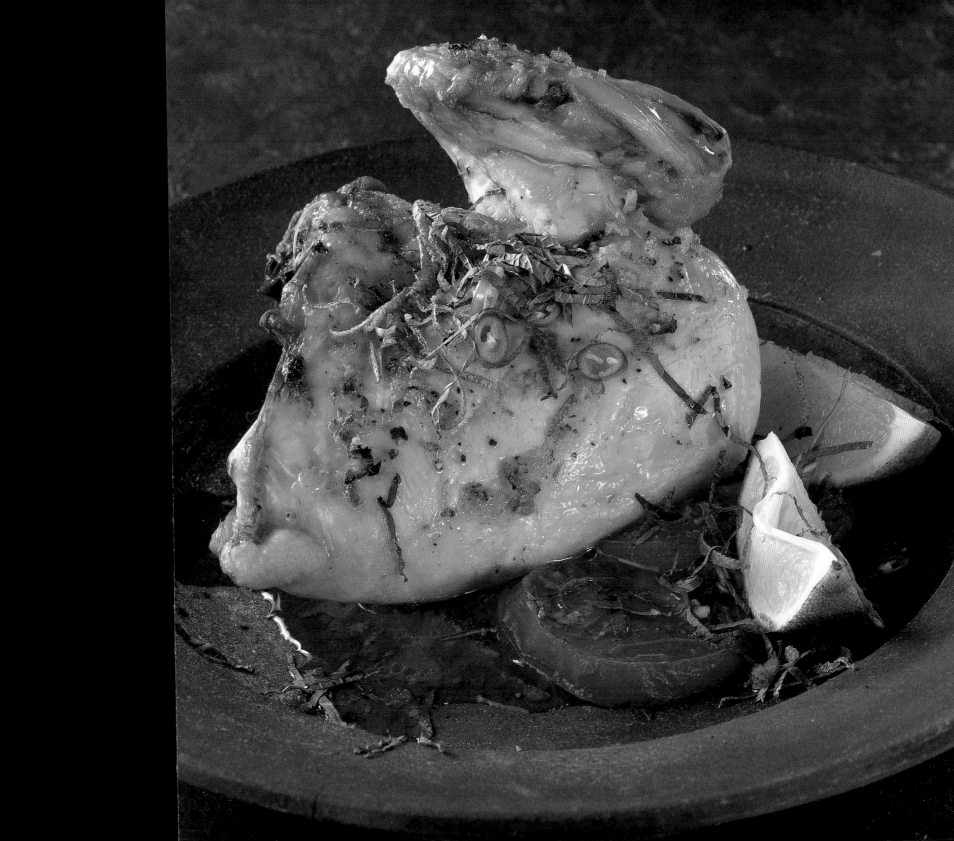

# GINGER AND LEMON CHICKEN

*This dish not only tastes wonderful but also looks very colourful when garnished with fresh cilantro, cherry tomatoes, and shredded ginger.*

SERVES 4

PREPARATION
*about 20 minutes*
COOKING
*15-20 minutes*

Calories per serving *127*
Total fat *4 g (25%)*
Saturated fat *2 g*
Protein *18 g*
Carbohydrate *7 g*
Cholesterol per serving
*48 mg*
Vitamins *A, B group, C, E*
Minerals *Calcium,*
*Potassium, Iron, Zinc,*
*Iodine*

**8 oz skinless boned chicken pieces**
**½ cup low-fat plain yogurt**
**2 tablespoons lemon juice**
**1½ teaspoons ginger pulp (page 17)**
**1 teaspoon dried crushed red chilies**
**1½ teaspoons ground coriander**
**½ teaspoon turmeric**
**salt**
**⅔ cup low-fat fromage blanc**
**1 tablespoon corn oil**

**1 bay leaf**
**8-10 mixed red and green peppercorns**
**2-3 green cardamom pods**
**1 tablespoon chopped fresh cilantro**

**for the garnish:**
**few sprigs fresh cilantro**
**8 cherry tomatoes, halved**
**1 tablespoon shredded ginger**

**1** Cut the chicken into cubes and set aside. In a medium mixing bowl, blend together the yogurt, lemon juice, ginger, dried crushed red chilies, ground coriander, turmeric, salt to taste and the fromage blanc. Mix everything together well and set aside

**2** In a frying pan, heat the corn oil with the bay leaf, mixed red and green peppercorns and cardamom pods over a moderate heat for about 2 minutes until aromatic. Pour in the yogurt and

spice mixture and cook for about 1 minute.

**3** Add the chicken, lower the heat, and cook for 7-10 minutes until the chicken is cooked through and lightly browned, stirring and checking occasionally to ensure that nothing is sticking to the bottom of the pan.

**4** Add the cilantro and stir for about 2 minutes, then transfer to a warmed serving dish.

**5** Garnish with the cilantro sprigs, tomatoes, and shredded ginger, and serve hot.

*Ginger and Lemon Chicken served with Rice with Desiccated Coconut (page 128)*

# ROASTED CHICKEN QUARTERS WITH SPICY HONEY SAUCE

*This chicken has a sauce that is sweet yet tangy, as it contains some tamarind. It can be served with Rice with Pine Nuts (page 128) and a vegetable stir-fry.*

SERVES 4

PREPARATION
*about 15 minutes*
COOKING
*about 45 minutes*

Calories per serving *280*
Total fat *10 g (31%)*
Saturated fat *2 g*
Protein *31 g*
Carbohydrate *19 g*
Cholesterol per serving
*113 mg*
Vitamins *B group, C, E*
Minerals *Potassium, Iron, Zinc, Selenium*

*1 chicken, about 2½-3¼ lbs*
*1 tablespoon tamarind pulp (see page 15)*
*2 tablespoons tomato purée*
*2 tablespoons honey*
*1 teaspoon ginger pulp (page 17)*
*1 teaspoon chili powder*
*1½ teaspoons ground coriander*
*salt*

*2 teaspoons sugar*
*2 tablespoons chopped fresh cilantro leaves*
*2 fresh red chilies, diced*
*heaping ½ cup canned chickpeas, drained*
*2 tablespoons corn oil*
*4-6 curry leaves*
*large pinch onion seeds*

**1**  Preheat the oven to 375°F. Prepare the chicken by removing the skin and cutting it into quarters.

**2**  In a bowl, mix the tamarind sauce, tomato purée, honey, ginger, chili powder, ground coriander, salt to taste, sugar, half of the cilantro, half of the red chilies, the chickpeas, and 1¼ cups water to form a thick paste.

**3**  Heat the oil in a saucepan over moderate heat. Add the curry leaves and onion seeds and fry for about 45 seconds. Pour in the honey sauce and cook for about 2 minutes. Remove from the heat.

**4**  Using a pastry brush, brush half of the sauce over the chicken pieces. Place the chicken in the oven for 35-40 minutes, basting occasionally, until golden and cooked through.

**5**  Serve with the remainder of the sauce poured over the top and garnished with the remaining cilantro and red chilies.

# STIR-FRIED CHICKEN WITH CILANTRO AND LEMON

SERVES 4

PREPARATION
*about 15 minutes*
COOKING
*about 15 minutes*

*8 oz skinless boned chicken*
*2 tablespoons corn oil*
*2 onions, sliced*
*½ teaspoon cumin seeds*
*8 curry leaves*
*3 garlic cloves*
*1½ teaspoons shredded ginger*
*1 teaspoon crushed dried red chilies*

*salt*
*1 tablespoon lemon juice*
*10-12 snow peas*
*2 oz corn kernels*
*2 fresh red chilies, seeded and sliced lengthwise*
*1 tablespoon finely chopped fresh cilantro leaves, plus more whole leaves, for garnish*

1 Cut the chicken into strips and set aside.

2 In a kadahi, wok, or deep frying pan, heat the oil over moderate heat. Add the onion, cumin seeds, and curry leaves, and fry for about 2 minutes until aromatic and the onions are softened.

3 Add the garlic, ginger, dried chilies, salt to taste, and lemon juice. Then add the chicken and turn the heat down slightly. Stir-fry for 5-7 minutes, until all the chicken pieces are cooked through.

4 Add the snow peas, corn, fresh chilies, and cilantro. Stir-fry for 2 to 3 minutes more before serving, garnished with some whole cilantro leaves.

Calories per serving *160*
Total fat *7 g (37%)*
Saturated fat *1 g*
Protein *16 g*
Carbohydrate *10 g*
Cholesterol per serving *39 mg*
Vitamins *A, B group, C, E*
Minerals *Potassium, Iron*

# CHICKEN BREASTS WITH FRUITY SAFFRON SAUCE

*Saffron—reputedly the most expensive spice in the world—has a beautiful aroma. In India and Pakistan it is used for special dishes. Here, a delicious saffron sauce is poured over chicken breasts with nuts and fruit.*

**4 chicken breast fillets, skinned**
**1 tablespoon tomato purée**
**3 tablespoons low-fat plain yogurt**
**1 teaspoon garlic pulp (page 17)**
**½ teaspoon garam masala**
**¼ teaspoon ground fennel seeds**
**¼ teaspoon ground cardamom seeds**
**4 tablespoons low-fat fromage blanc**
**1 teaspoon ground almonds**

**½ teaspoon chili powder**
**1 tablespoon lemon juice**
**salt**
**¼ teaspoon saffron threads**
**1 tablespoon corn oil**
**1 bay leaf**
**1 cinnamon stick**
**2 tablespoons golden raisins**
**1 tablespoon sliced almonds**

SERVES 4

PREPARATION *about 15 minutes, plus 1 hour marinating*
COOKING *20-25 minutes*

Calories per serving *217*
Total fat *11 g (46%)*
Saturated fat *2 g*
Protein *22 g*
Carbohydrate *8 g*
Cholesterol per serving *56 mg*
Vitamins *B group, C, E*
Minerals *Potassium, Iron, Selenium*

1 Using a sharp knife, make 2 slashes into each chicken breast without cutting right through. This will help the flavors and heat to penetrate. Place the chicken in a heatproof dish.

2 In a small bowl, blend together the tomato purée, yogurt, garlic, garam masala, fennel, cardamom, fromage blanc, ground almonds, chili powder, lemon juice, salt to taste, and the saffron with 4 tablespoons water.

3 Heat the oil in a deep frying pan. Add the bay leaf and cinnamon stick and fry for about 30 seconds until aromatic. Add the sauce mixture together with ⅔ cup water and bring to a boil. Pour over the top of the chicken breasts and leave to marinate for about 1 hour.

4 Preheat the oven to 375°F. Sprinkle the raisins and almonds over the chicken. Cook in the preheated oven for 15-20 minutes until the chicken is firm and cooked through.

# TANDOORI CHICKEN WITH RADISH SALAD

*Tandoori chicken is probably one of the most popular of all dishes from the subcontinent. Ideally it should be cooked in a clay oven (the tandoor), though an oven preheated to its highest possible temperature produces satisfying results as well.*

SERVES 4

PREPARATION
*about 15 minutes,
plus 3 hours
marinating*
COOKING
*15-18 minutes*

Calories per serving *229*
Total fat *5 g (19%)*
Saturated fat *1 g*
Protein *38 g*
Carbohydrate *10 g*
Cholesterol per serving
*137 mg*
Vitamins *A, B group, C, E*
Minerals *Calcium,
Potassium, Iron, Zinc,
Selenium, Iodine*

**1 chicken, about 3¼ lbs**
**⅔ cup low-fat plain yogurt**
**1 teaspoon ginger pulp (page 17)**
**1 teaspoon garlic pulp (page 17)**
**1 tablespoon tomato purée**
**1 teaspoon paprika**
**2 tablespoons lemon juice**
**1½ teaspoons ground coriander**
**1 teaspoon garam masala**
**salt**

**corn oil, for greasing baking tray**
**lemon or lime wedges, for serving**

**for the radish salad:**
**4 large leaves iceberg lettuce, shredded**
**1 red onion, thinly sliced**
**½ cucumber, peeled and sliced**
**2 tomatoes, quartered**
**4 whole green chilies**
**4 oz radishes or mooli (page 20), sliced**

**1** Skin the chicken and cut it into 8 pieces. Using a sharp knife, make 2 deep slashes in each piece without cutting right through, to allow flavors and heat to penetrate the flesh.

**2** Pour the yogurt into a large bowl. Add the ginger, garlic, tomato purée, paprika, lemon juice, ground coriander, garam masala, salt to taste, and 1 cup water. Mix well and pour over the chicken pieces. Leave to marinate for at least 3 hours or overnight.

**3** When ready to cook, preheat the oven to its highest possible temperature. Lift the chicken pieces from the marinade, place them on a greased

baking tray, and place in the hot oven. Cook the chicken for 15-18 minutes, checking once or twice to make sure it is not browning too fast (if burn marks begin to appear too rapidly, just turn the oven down slightly), until the juices run clear (not pink) when the thickest part of the flesh is poked with the tip of a knife.

**4** While the chicken is cooking, make the salad by mixing all the ingredients, then arranging on 4 serving plates.

**5** Serve the chicken with the salad and lemon or lime wedges.

*Tandoori Chicken with Radish Salad*

# SPAGHETTI WITH MINI CHICKEN KOFTA

*Although it may not seem authentic, spaghetti was always a great favorite of mine as a child living in Pakistan, only my mother prepared it in her own unique way. This is my version of that childhood staple.*

**for the kofta:**
10 oz skinless boned chicken, cubed
1½ teaspoons ginger pulp (page 17)
1½ teaspoons garlic pulp (page 17)
1 teaspoon ground cumin
2 teaspoons ground coriander
1 teaspoon chili powder
1 teaspoon mango powder
salt
2 tablespoons chopped fresh cilantro leaves
1 fresh red chili, diced
1 small egg, lightly beaten
2 tablespoons corn oil

**for the spiced tomato sauce:**
4 tablespoons tomato purée

2 tablespoons low-fat fromage blanc
1 teaspoon ground coriander
1 teaspoon garlic pulp (page 17)
1 teaspoon ginger pulp (page 17)
1 teaspoon chili powder
salt
1 tablespoon corn oil
4 curry leaves
¼ teaspoon onion seeds

**for the garnish:**
1 fresh red chili, chopped
few fresh mint leaves, shredded
freshly ground black peppercorns

8 oz spaghetti

SERVES 4

PREPARATION
*about 25 minutes*
COOKING
*about 30 minutes*

Calories per serving *266*
Total fat *13 g (44%)*
Saturated fat *3 g*
Protein *22 g*
Carbohydrate *18 g*
Cholesterol per serving
*122 mg*
Vitamins *A, B group, C, E*
Minerals *Calcium,
Potassium, Iron, Zinc,
Selenium, Iodine*

**1** To prepare the kofta, combine the chicken, ginger, garlic, cumin, coriander, chili powder, mango powder, and salt to taste. Place in a saucepan and pour in 2½ cups water. Bring to a boil, lower the heat and cook for 12-15 minutes, until the liquid has fully evaporated and the chicken pieces are cooked. Allow to cool.

**2** When the chicken is cool, process it in a food processor with the cilantro and chili until minced.

**3** Bind the chicken mixture together by adding the beaten egg. Break off golf-ball-size pieces and mold them into rounds (about 20-25).

**4** Heat the oil in a small frying pan (preferably non-stick). Add the koftas and fry for 4-6 minutes until golden brown all over. Remove from the heat and set aside.

**5** To make the sauce, in a medium bowl, combine the tomato purée, fromage blanc, coriander, garlic, ginger, chili, salt to taste, and ⅔ cup water. Heat the oil in a saucepan over moderate heat with the curry leaves and onion seeds. Lower the heat and pour in the sauce. Bring to a boil and cook for an additional minute. Add the cooked koftas to the sauce and keep warm.

**6** Cook the spaghetti in a large pan of boiling salted water until just tender. Drain.

**7** Pour the sauce over the spaghetti and serve with the garnish.

*Spaghetti with Mini Chicken Kofta*

# CHICKEN WITH FENUGREEK AND TOMATOES

*Chicken goes extremely well with fenugreek and tomatoes. Fenugreek has a beautiful aroma and the tomato base gives this curry a rich flavor.*

SERVES 4

PREPARATION
*about 25 minutes*
COOKING
*about 20 minutes*

Calories per serving *194*
Total fat *11 g (52%)*
Saturated fat *2 g*
Protein *15 g*
Carbohydrate *10 g*
Cholesterol per serving
*51 mg*
Vitamins *A, B group, C, E*
Minerals *Potassium, Iron, Zinc*

**8 oz skinless boned chicken**
**3 tablespoons fresh fenugreek**
**1 tablespoon sesame seeds**
**1 tablespoon tamarind paste**
**1 teaspoon chili powder**
**salt**
**1 teaspoon ground coriander**
**½ teaspoon ground cumin**
**1 teaspoon ginger pulp (page 17)**

**1 teaspoon garlic pulp (page 17)**
**2 teaspoons sugar**
**2 tablespoons corn oil**
**¼ teaspoon mixed fenugreek seeds and onion seeds**
**4-6 curry leaves**
**6 tomatoes, coarsely chopped**
**2 tablespoons fresh cilantro leaves**
**1 fresh green chili, chopped**

**1** Cut the chicken into cubes and set aside. Break the leaves off the fresh fenugreek, wash them, and pat dry.

**2** Place the sesame seeds in a spice grinder and grind to a fine powder. Place the powder in a small bowl and add the tamarind, chili, salt to taste, coriander, cumin, ginger, garlic, and sugar. Using a spoon, mix with about 2 tablespoons water.

**3** Heat the oil and the mixed fenugreek and onion seeds and the curry leaves over moderate heat in a kadahi, wok, or deep frying pan for about 1 minute until aromatic. Add the tomatoes, followed by the spice paste. Stir to mix everything together, then add the chicken pieces. Stir-fry for 2 minutes.

**4** Add the fenugreek leaves, lower the heat, cover, and cook for 10 minutes, stirring occasionally.

**5** Remove the lid and stir in the chili and one tablespoon of the cilantro. Cook for an additional 2 minutes and serve hot, garnished with the remaining cilantro.

*Chicken with Fenugreek and Tomatoes*

# CHICKEN KADAHI

Kadahi, *wok-like utensils with a ring-shaped handle on each side, are used for stir-frying and deep-frying. Traditionally they were made of cast iron, but nowadays they are also available in stainless steel, making them attractive enough to serve from at the dining table.*

SERVES 4

PREPARATION
*about 15 minutes*
COOKING
*20-25 minutes*

Calories per serving *153*
Total fat *7 g (43%)*
Saturated fat *1 g*
Protein *14 g*
Carbohydrate *8 g*
Cholesterol per serving
*51 mg*
Vitamins *B group, C, E*
Minerals *Potassium, Iron, Zinc*

**8 oz skinless boned chicken**
**2 tablespoons corn oil**
**2 onions, diced**
**1 teaspoon garlic pulp (page 17)**
**1 teaspoon ginger pulp (page 17)**
**1 teaspoon ground coriander**
**1 teaspoon chili powder**

**salt**
**2 tablespoons chopped fresh cilantro leaves**
**1 green bell pepper, seeded and sliced**
**8 cherry tomatoes**
**½ teaspoon garam masala**
**1 teaspoon shredded ginger, for garnish**
**1 lime, cut in wedges, for serving**

**1**  Cut the chicken into bite-sized cubes and set aside.

**2**  Heat the oil over moderate heat in a kadahi, wok, or deep frying pan. Add the onions and fry for about 3 minutes until softened.

**3**  Add the chicken pieces and stir-fry until firm.

**4**  Add the garlic, ginger, coriander, chili powder, and salt to taste and continue to stir-fry for an additional 2 minutes. Add half the cilantro and

about 1½ cups water. Reduce the heat slightly and cook for 7-10 minutes, until the sauce begins to thicken and the chicken is cooked. Add the bell pepper, cherry tomatoes, and garam masala, and stir-fry for an additional 2 minutes.

**5**  Serve garnished with the shredded ginger and remaining cilantro. Squeeze the juice from a wedge of the lime over the chicken and serve with the remaining lime wedges.

# LAMB KEBABS WITH SPICY GINGER FILLING

*These fruity delicious kebabs can also be made with ground beef if you prefer.*

*1 lb lean ground lamb*
*1 teaspoon ground cumin*
*1 teaspoon ground coriander*
*1 teaspoon garam masala*
*1 teaspoon ginger pulp (page 17)*
*1 teaspoon garlic pulp (page 17)*
*¼ teaspoon ground cardamom seeds*
*1 teaspoon chili powder*
*1 tablespoon chopped fresh cilantro leaves*
*2 tablespoons chopped fresh mint*
*1 small onion, diced*

*salt*
*corn oil, for frying kebabs*

*for the filling:*
*1 tablespoon shredded ginger*
*1 fresh green chili, seeded and chopped*
*1 fresh red chili, seeded and chopped*
*2 tablespoons chopped fresh cilantro leaves*
*2 tablespoons low-fat plain yogurt*
*2 medium tomatoes, seeded and diced*

SERVES 4
(MAKES 10-12)

PREPARATION
*about 30 minutes*
COOKING
*about 20 minutes*

Calories per serving *200*
Total fat *11 g (46%)*
Saturated fat *5 g*
Protein *24 g*
Carbohydrate *5 g*
Cholesterol per serving
*84 mg*
Vitamins *A, B group, C, E*
Minerals *Potassium, Iron, Zinc, Iodine*

1   Place the ground lamb, ground cumin, ground coriander, garam masala, ginger, garlic, cardamom, chili powder, cilantro, mint, onion, and salt to taste in a saucepan.

2   Using a fork or your hands, mix everything together thoroughly. Pour in 5 tablespoons water, bring to a simmer, and cook over low heat, stirring occasionally, for 10-12 minutes, until the liquid has evaporated. Then stir continuously until completely dry, and remove from the heat. Set aside to cool.

3   To make the filling, combine all of the ingredients in a medium bowl. Set aside.

4   Place the meat mixture in a food processor and process for 1-1½ minutes, until quite pasty. Transfer to a bowl and use your hands to mix together well. Break off small balls and shape them into flat rounds in the palm of your hand. Make a dimple in the middle with your thumb, fill this with about 1 teaspoon of the filling mix, and fold the sides over to enclose the filling and make a flat round shape again. Place on a tray. Repeat until you have made 10-12 kebabs.

5   Brush a nonstick frying pan with a little oil and gently fry the kebabs in batches, pressing them down with a spatula, for about 40 seconds on each side. Alternatively, lightly brush the kebabs with oil and broil.

# HARA MASALA LAMB KEBABS

*Hara masala means "green spices"—here, scallions, cilantro, and green chilies. These kebabs are excellent for picnics, as you can serve them sandwiched in buns like burgers. (See page 65.)*

SERVES 4

PREPARATION
*about 30 minutes*
COOKING
*15-20 minutes*

Calories per serving *269*
Total fat *18 g (62%)*
Saturated fat *6 g*
Protein *25 g*
Carbohydrate *1 g*
Cholesterol per serving
*141 mg*
Vitamins *B group, C, E*
Minerals *Potassium, Iron,
Zinc, Iodine*

*1 lb lean ground lamb*
*4 scallions, chopped*
*2 tablespoons chopped fresh cilantro leaves*
*1 tablespoon chopped fresh mint plus more sprigs
for garnish*
*2-3 fresh green chilies, chopped*

*1 teaspoon shredded ginger*
*1 teaspoon garlic pulp (page 17)*
*salt*
*1 small egg, lightly beaten*
*2-3 tablespoons corn oil*
*a few leaves of chicory for garnish*

**1** Place the lamb in a food processor and process it for about 30 seconds to get a finer texture. Add the scallions, cilantro, mint, chilies, ginger, garlic, and salt to taste. Process for about 1 minute more.

**2** Remove the mixture from the processor and place in a bowl. Blend in the egg and mix well, using either your fingers or a fork.

**3** Break off small balls of the mixture and make them into 12-16 flat round shapes in your palm.

**4** When all the kebabs are made, heat half the oil in a nonstick frying pan over moderate heat. Add half the kebabs and fry slowly, turning twice and pressing them down as they cook, until well browned, 6-8 minutes. As the kebabs are cooked, remove them from the pan and drain on paper towels to absorb any excess oil. Cook the remaining kebabs in the same way.

**5** Serve garnished with chicory and mint sprigs.

# LAMB PULAO

SERVES 4

PREPARATION
*about 30 minutes,
plus 1 hour
marinating*
COOKING
*about 45 minutes,
plus 5 minutes
standing*

*1 lb lean boned leg of lamb, cut into strips about
¼ inch thick and 2 inches long*
*1¼ cups low-fat plain yogurt*
*2 tablespoons ground almonds*
*¼ teaspoon ground cardamom seeds*
*1 teaspoon chili powder*
*1 teaspoon garam masala*
*1 teaspoon ginger pulp (page 17)*
*1 teaspoon garlic pulp (page 17)*
*1 tablespoon desiccated coconut*
*3 tablespoons chopped fresh cilantro leaves*

*3-4 tablespoons corn oil*
*2 onions, sliced*
*2 oz green beans, cut into short lengths*
*2 fresh tomatoes, chopped*
*1 bay leaf*
*2 cups rice, washed*
*1 fresh green chili, chopped*
*1 fresh red chili, chopped*
*3 tablespoons lemon juice*
*½ teaspoon saffron threads*

*Previous pages: Lamb Chops with Grilled Vegetables, Lamb Pulao served with Chapati (page 124)*

1   Place the lamb in a large bowl and add the yogurt, ground almonds, ground cardamom, chili powder, garam masala, ginger, garlic, coconut, and 1 tablespoon of the cilantro. Blend everything together and set aside to marinate for about 1 hour.

2   Heat the oil in a large saucepan over moderate heat. Add the onions and fry until golden brown. Add the beans, tomatoes, bay leaf, and lamb mixture. Bring to a simmer, lower the heat and cook, covered, for 7-10 minutes, stirring occasionally.

3   Pour in the rice and stir it gently with a slotted spoon. Add the remaining cilantro, the green and red chilies, lemon juice, and saffron. Pour in 3 cups water and bring to a boil. Lower the heat, cover with a lid, and cook for 10-15 minutes, until the water is fully absorbed and the rice is cooked.

4   Leave the dish to stand off the heat for about 5 minutes before serving.

Calories per serving *592*
Total fat *27 g (41%)*
Saturated fat *9 g*
Protein *32 g*
Carbohydrate *59 g*
Cholesterol per serving *85 mg*
Vitamins *A, B group, C, E*
Minerals *Potassium, Iron, Zinc, Iodine*

# LAMB CHOPS WITH GRILLED VEGETABLES

*I use a grill pan just to brown the chops and then finish them in the oven for about 20 minutes.*

**8 lamb chops, each 3-4½ oz**
**2 teaspoons garlic pulp (page 17)**
**2 teaspoons ginger pulp (page 17)**
**2 fresh green chilies, finely chopped**
**4 tablespoons chopped fresh cilantro leaves**
**salt**
**3 tablespoons lemon juice**
**1 tablespoon cornstarch**
**corn oil, for brushing the pan**

**1 lime, quartered, for serving**

**for the grilled vegetables:**
**1 tablespoon olive oil**
**1 red onion, thickly sliced**
**1 green bell pepper, seeded and quartered**
**2 firm plum tomatoes, halved**
**1 zucchini, thickly sliced at an angle**
**½ teaspoon crushed dried red chilies**

SERVES 4

PREPARATION
*about 25 minutes, plus 1 hour marinating*
COOKING
*about 20 minutes*

1   Trim the chops well by removing all the fat.

2   In a small bowl, mix together the garlic, ginger, chilies, 3 tablespoons of the cilantro, salt to taste, lemon juice, cornstarch, and 2 tablespoons water. Place the chops on a plate and rub them all over with this mixture. Leave to marinate for about 1 hour.

3   Preheat the oven to 375°F and a ridged grill pan over moderate heat. Brush the pan lightly with the corn oil. Place the chops in the pan and grill for about 1 minute on each side. Transfer them to an ovenproof dish and grill the remaining chops in the same way. Cook the chops in the oven for 15-20 minutes, until cooked to taste.

4   About 10 minutes before the lamb is ready, preheat the grill pan again for the vegetables. Brush lightly with olive oil and start cooking, pressing down on them to get a char-grilled effect. Sprinkle with salt to taste and the crushed dried red chilies.

5   Remove the chops from the oven and serve with the vegetables alongside, garnished with the remaining cilantro, and the lime quarters.

Calories per serving *238*
Total fat *12 g (47%)*
Saturated fat *4 g*
Protein *22 g*
Carbohydrate *10 g*
Cholesterol per serving *74 mg*
Vitamins *A, B group, C, E*
Minerals *Potassium, Iron, Zinc*

# STIR-FRIED STRIPS OF LAMB WITH PEPPERS AND PINEAPPLE

*I feel lamb cut into strips is much quicker and easier to cook than the cubes traditional in Indian cuisine. You can use fresh pineapple, or good-quality canned pineapple in juice (not syrup).*

SERVES 4

PREPARATION
*about 20 minutes,
plus 30 minutes
marinating*
COOKING
*about 20 minutes*

Calories per serving *203*
Total fat *13 g (60%)*
Saturated fat *3 g*
Protein *13 g*
Carbohydrate *10 g*
Cholesterol per serving
*42 mg*
Vitamins *A, B group, C, E*
Minerals *Potassium, Iron,
Zinc*

**8 oz boned lamb**
**1 teaspoon ground coriander**
**1 teaspoon ground cumin**
**1 teaspoon mango powder**
**½ cup pineapple juice**
**1 teaspoon hot chili sauce**
**1 teaspoon garlic pulp (page 17)**
**1 teaspoon ginger pulp (page 17)**
**¼ teaspoon turmeric**

**salt**
**2 tablespoons corn oil**
**½ red bell pepper, seeded and cubed**
**½ green bell pepper, seeded and cubed**
**12 pineapple chunks**
**1 tablespoon chopped fresh cilantro leaves, plus
more sprigs for garnish**
**1 tablespoon sesame seeds**

**1**  Prepare the lamb by trimming off any excess fat and cutting it into strips about 2 inches long and ¼ inch thick. Place in a mixing bowl.

**2**  Add to the lamb the ground coriander, cumin, mango powder, pineapple juice, chili sauce, garlic, ginger, turmeric, and salt to taste. Blend everything together, then set aside for about 30 minutes.

**3**  Heat the oil over moderate heat in a kadahi, wok, or deep frying pan. Drop the lamb into the oil and stir-fry for 2-3 minutes. Add about ⅔ cup water and bring to a simmer. Lower the heat, cover the pan, and cook gently for 7-10 minutes, stirring occasionally.

**4**  Add the cubed peppers followed by the pineapple chunks and the cilantro. Continue to stir-fry for an additional 2 minutes.

**5**  Garnish with the cilantro sprigs and sesame seeds to serve.

*Stir-Fried Strips of Lamb with Peppers and Pineapple*

# Vegetarian Dishes

# MASOOR DHAL KHICHERI WITH VEGETABLES

*Khicheri means rice cooked with lentils or other pulses. I have added vegetables to this version, which makes it a lot more interesting and tasty.*

SERVES 4-6

PREPARATION
*about 20 minutes*
COOKING
*25-30 minutes,
plus 5 minutes
standing*

Calories per serving *407*
Total fat *7 g (16%)*
Saturated fat *1 g*
Protein *15 g*
Carbohydrate *72 g*
Cholesterol per serving
*None*
Vitamins *A, B₁, B₃, B₆,*
*Folate, C, E*
Minerals *Potassium, Iron,*
*Zinc*

*2 cups basmati rice*
*1 cup masoor dhal (salmon-colored lentils,*
*page 23)*
*2 tablespoons corn oil*
*4-6 curry leaves*
*¼ teaspoon mixed mustard seeds and onion seeds*
*1 small onion, sliced*
*1 teaspoon ginger pulp (page 17)*

*1 teaspoon garlic pulp (page 17)*
*½ teaspoon turmeric*
*1 medium carrot, diced*
*2 oz shelled peas*
*2 oz green beans, sliced into short lengths*
*salt*
*1 tablespoon chopped fresh cilantro leaves, plus
more sprigs, for garnish*

**1**  Wash the rice and masoor dhal well and leave in a bowl of water to soak.

**2**  Heat the oil in a medium-sized heavy-bottomed saucepan. Add the curry leaves, mustard and onion seeds, and onion, and fry for about 2 minutes until aromatic and the onion is softened.

**3**  Lower the heat and add the ginger, garlic, turmeric, carrot, peas, green beans, and salt to taste. Drain the water from the rice and lentils and

add to the spiced onion mixture. Stir for about 2 minutes, then add 4 cups water. Stir gently and add the cilantro. When the water begins to boil, lower heat, cover the pan, and cook for 15-20 minutes.

**4**  Leave to stand off the heat, still covered, for 5 minutes before serving, garnished with cilantro sprigs.

# ZUCCHINI AND EGGPLANT IN A MINTY YOGURT SAUCE

SERVES 4

PREPARATION
*about 25 minutes*
COOKING
*25-30 minutes*

*1 medium eggplant*
*1¼ cups low-fat plain yogurt*
*1 teaspoon mint sauce*
*1 tablespoon chopped fresh mint*
*1 teaspoon sugar*
*salt*
*2 fresh red chilies, chopped*

*1 tablespoon corn oil*
*6 curry leaves*
*¼ teaspoon white cumin seeds*
*1 large zucchini, sliced*
*1 tablespoon chopped fresh cilantro leaves, for
garnish*

*Previous pages: Okra with New Potatoes, Masoor Dhal Khicheri with Vegetables*

**1**   Preheat the oven to 375°F. Cut the top off the eggplant and bake it in the oven for 20-25 minutes. When it is cool enough to handle, remove the skin and mash the flesh down with a fork.

**2**   In a large bowl, whisk the yogurt and mix it with the eggplant flesh, mint sauce, fresh mint, sugar, salt to taste, and red chilies. Set aside.

**3**   Heat the oil in a kadahi, wok, or deep frying pan. Add the curry leaves, white cumin seeds, and zucchini, and stir-fry for 1-1½ minutes over moderate heat.

**4**   Pour the zucchini and their seasoned oil over the top of the yogurt and eggplant mixture. Garnish with the cilantro to serve.

Calories per serving *85*
Total fat *4 g (40%)*
Saturated fat *1 g*
Protein *5 g*
Carbohydrate *9 g*
Cholesterol per serving *3 mg*
Vitamins *A, B₂, B₃, B₆, B₁₂, Folate, C*
Minerals *Calcium, Iron, Iodine*

# OKRA WITH NEW POTATOES

*1 lb okra*
*10 new potatoes*
*salt*
*2 tablespoons corn oil*
*3 onions, sliced*
*large pinch onion seeds*
*large pinch fennel seeds*
*large pinch mustard seeds*

*½ teaspoon crushed dried red chilies*
*4 garlic cloves, sliced*
*2 tomatoes, quartered*
*2 tablespoons chopped fresh cilantro leaves, plus more leaves, for garnish*
*1 fresh green chili, chopped*
*1 teaspoon lemon juice*

SERVES 4

PREPARATION
*about 15 minutes*
COOKING
*25-30 minutes*

Calories per serving *220*
Total fat *7 g (31%)*
Saturated fat *1 g*
Protein *7 g*
Carbohydrate *33 g*
Cholesterol per serving *None*
Vitamins *A, B₁, B₃, B₆, Folate, C, E*
Minerals *Calcium, Potassium, Iron, Zinc*

**1**   Cut the okra and potatoes in half. Cook the potatoes in boiling salted water until just soft but not mushy. Drain and set aside.

**2**   In a heavy-bottomed saucepan over a moderate heat, fry the onions with the mixed seeds in the oil for 3-4 minutes, or until the onions are golden.

**3**   Add the crushed chilies, followed by the garlic, and stir-fry for about 1 minute. Then add the tomatoes, okra, cilantro, fresh green chili, lemon juice, and salt to taste. Lower the heat slightly, cover the pan and cook for 5-7 minutes.

**4**   Add the potato halves, cover again, and cook for an additional 3-5 minutes. Serve garnished with more cilantro.

# LENTILS COOKED WITH VEGETABLES AND TAMARIND

*Eaten widely in southern India, this lentil dish should ideally be served with rice or* poori *(deep-fried bread). It can also be served in small bowls, as people drink it like a soup with their meal.*

SERVES 4

PREPARATION
*about 20 minutes*
COOKING
*40-45 minutes*

Calories per serving *150*
Total fat *5 g (30%)*
Saturated fat *1 g*
Protein *4 g*
Carbohydrate *24 g*
Cholesterol per serving
*None*
Vitamins *A, B₁, B₃, B₆,*
*Folate, C, E*
Minerals *Potassium, Iron*

*2 tablespoons toor dhal (page 23)*
*2 tablespoons masoor dhal (page 23)*
*1 teaspoon ginger pulp (page 17)*
*1 teaspoon garlic pulp (page 17)*
*½ teaspoon turmeric*
*1 teaspoon chili powder*
*1 heaping teaspoon ground coriander*
*salt*
*1 onion, chopped*
*3 curry leaves*
*1 oz green beans, cut into pieces*

*1 carrot, diced*
*1 potato, diced*
*1 tablespoon tamarind paste*
*1 tablespoon brown sugar*
*2 tablespoons chopped fresh cilantro leaves*

*for the tarka (seasoned oil):*
*1-2 tablespoons corn oil*
*½ teaspoon mustard seeds*
*3 whole dried red chilies*
*4-6 curry leaves*

**1** Mix together the two dhals and wash them twice, running your fingers through them.

**2** Drain and put in a heavy-bottomed saucepan. Add the ginger, garlic, turmeric, chili powder, ground coriander, salt to taste, onion, and curry leaves, followed by 2½ cups water. Bring to a boil, lower the heat and cook, partly covered, for 10-15 minutes, stirring occasionally. Check to see if the lentils have absorbed all the water; if they have, add more—up to 1¼ cups—and cook until the lentils are mushy enough to be mashed down to a paste, about 20-25 minutes.

**3** Add the green beans, carrots, and potato, followed by an additional 1¼ cups water. Cook over low heat for an additional 5-7 minutes.

**4** When the vegetables are cooked, add the tamarind paste, sugar, and half the cilantro, followed by another 1¼ cups water. Stir and bring to a boil. Remove from the heat and transfer to a warmed serving dish.

**5** To make the tarka, heat the oil in a frying pan over moderate heat. Add the mustard seeds, dried red chilies, and curry leaves. When the oil is hot and smoky, pour the tarka over the lentils.

**6** Serve garnished with the remaining cilantro.

*Lentils Cooked with Vegetables and Tamarind*

# VEGETABLE AND RED KIDNEY BEAN PULAO

*This pulao makes an excellent complete vegetarian meal.*

*2 cups basmati rice*
*5 oz canned red kidney beans*
*2 tablespoons corn oil*
*1 cinnamon stick*
*1 bay leaf*
*2 cloves*
*3 green cardamom pods*
*4 black peppercorns*
*1 onion, sliced*
*1 teaspoon ginger pulp (page 17)*
*1 teaspoon garlic pulp (page 17)*
*1 teaspoon chili powder*
*½ teaspoon turmeric*
*1 teaspoon garam masala*
*1 teaspoon ground coriander seeds*
*2 oz shelled peas*
*2 oz cauliflower florets*
*1 carrot, sliced*
*1 zucchini, sliced*
*2 tablespoons low-fat plain yogurt*
*salt*
*2 tablespoons chopped fresh cilantro leaves*
*2 fresh red chilies, sliced*
*1 tablespoon lemon juice*

SERVES 4

PREPARATION
*about 25 minutes*
COOKING
*about 25 minutes,
plus 5 minutes
resting*

Calories per serving *331*
Total fat *7 g (19%)*
Saturated fat *1 g*
Protein *10 g*
Carbohydrate *58 g*
Cholesterol per serving
*None*
Vitamins *A, B₁, B₃, B₆,
Folate, C, E*
Minerals *Potassium, Iron*

1   Wash the rice until the water runs clear. Leave to soak while you prepare the other ingredients. Drain the liquid from the kidney beans and set aside.

2   In a large heavy-bottomed saucepan, heat the corn oil over moderate heat. Add the cinnamon stick, bay leaf, cloves, cardamom pods, and peppercorns, and cook for about 1 minute. Add the onions and fry for about 2 minutes until softened.

3   Lower the heat and add the ginger, garlic, chili powder, turmeric, garam masala, and ground coriander, followed by all the vegetables. Stir-fry for about 2 minutes, stirring in the yogurt toward the end of that time.

4   Drain the rice and add it and the beans to the pan. Using a slotted spoon, gently stir to mix well without breaking up the rice. Add salt to taste, half the cilantro, the red chilies, lemon juice, and 3 cups water. Bring to a boil, then turn the heat down to moderate. Cover the pan with a lid and cook until the water has been absorbed and the rice is cooked, about 10-15 minutes.

5   Let the pulao sit, covered, for about 5 minutes off the heat before serving, garnished with the remaining cilantro.

*Vegetable and Red Kidney Bean Pulao*

# EGGPLANT WITH TOMATO AND ONION

*Eggplant is very popular in Indian cooking and is used in a variety of ways. This particular recipe goes very well with freshly made chapatis (page 124) and Mango and Apple Chutney (page 139).*

SERVES 4

PREPARATION
*about 20 minutes*
COOKING
*about 15 minutes*

Calories per serving *105*
Total fat *6 g (54%)*
Saturated fat *1 g*
Protein *3 g*
Carbohydrate *11 g*
Cholesterol per serving
*None*
Vitamins *B₃, B₆, Folate, C, E*
Minerals *Potassium, Iron*

*1 large eggplant*
*2 onions*
*2 tablespoons corn oil*
*large pinch mustard seeds*
*4 curry leaves*
*1 tablespoon tomato purée*
*1 tablespoon ground coriander*

*1 teaspoon garlic pulp (page 17)*
*1 teaspoon ginger pulp (page 17)*
*salt*
*1 tablespoon lemon juice*
*1 tablespoon chopped fresh cilantro leaves*
*2 firm tomatoes, seeded and diced*
*1 fresh green chili, chopped*

**1**  Wash the eggplant, cut it into very small pieces, and place in a bowl. Chop the onions very finely.

**2**  Heat the oil in a medium saucepan over moderate heat and add the mustard seeds, curry leaves, and onions. Lower the heat and add the tomato purée, followed by the ground coriander, garlic, ginger, salt to taste, and lemon juice, stirring continuously. Cook, stirring, for 3-5 minutes, until aromatic and the onions are softened.

**3**  Add the eggplant and continue to stir-fry for an additional 2 minutes. Stir in ⅔ cup water, cover, and cook over low heat for 5-7 minutes, stirring occasionally.

**4**  Add the fresh cilantro and tomatoes, followed by the green chili. Stir gently for a minute or so, then serve.

*Eggplant with Tomato and Onion served with Mango and Apple Chutney (page 139) and Chapati (page 124)*

# BROILED VEGETABLES IN A PANCAKE ROLL

*Broiled vegetables have become very popular in the last few years. I serve them in a spicy pancake roll, either as snacks or in large quantities with a salad for a main meal.*

SERVES 4

PREPARATION
*25-30 minutes,
plus 30 minutes
standing*
COOKING
*about 30 minutes*

Calories per serving *382*
Total fat *12 g (29%)*
Saturated fat *4 g*
Protein *14 g*
Carbohydrate *52 g*
Cholesterol per serving
*183 mg*
Vitamins *A, B group, C, E*
Minerals *Potassium, Iron*

*1 red onion, sliced*
*1 large green bell pepper, seeded and sliced*
*1 large orange bell pepper, seeded and sliced*
*1 zucchini, sliced*
*2 tomatoes, sliced*
*1 tablespoon olive oil*
*1 teaspoon fresh fenugreek*
*4 curry leaves*
*1 teaspoon crushed dried red chilies*
*salt*

*for the raita:*
*1 cup low-fat plain yogurt*
*2 tablespoons honey*

*2 fresh red chilies, chopped*
*2 tablespoons chopped fresh cilantro leaves*
*1 tablespoon chopped fresh mint*
*½ cucumber, diced*

*for the pancakes:*
*1½ cups all-purpose flour*
*3 medium-sized eggs*
*1½ cups low-fat milk*
*2 fresh chilies (1 red and 1 green), chopped*
*1 teaspoon ground pomegranate seeds*
*½ teaspoon ground cumin seeds*
*1 teaspoon chopped fresh cilantro leaves*
*1 tablespoon low-fat margarine*

**1** Prepare all the vegetables and set aside on a heatproof dish. Preheat the broiler.

**2** Heat the oil in a small saucepan and add the fenugreek, curry leaves, crushed dried red chilies, and a little salt. Stir-fry over moderate heat for about 1 minute. Set aside.

**3** Brush the vegetables with the seasoned oil and broil for 12-15 minutes until they begin to get lightly browned. Remove from the heat.

**4** To make the raita, whisk the yogurt using a small fork. Stir in the honey, followed by the remaining ingredients. Set aside in a serving bowl.

**5** To make the pancakes, sift the flour and a large pinch of salt into a large bowl. Beat the eggs well, then add them to the flour. Continue beating and gradually stir in the milk.

**6** Add the chilies, followed by the pomegranate seeds, cumin, and cilantro. Blend together well and let the batter stand for about 30 minutes.

**7** Heat ½ teaspoon of the margarine in a 10-inch nonstick frying pan over moderate heat. Pour in about one-quarter of the pancake batter, tilting the pan so the batter spreads well and coats the bottom of the pan evenly.

**8** When you see fine bubbles begin to appear on top of the pancake, flip it over with a spatula and cook for a minute or so on the other side. Transfer the cooked pancake to a plate and keep warm. Cook the remaining pancakes in the same way.

**9** Roll some of the filling up in each of the pancakes and serve with the remaining vegetables and the raita.

*Broiled Vegetables in a Pancake Roll*

# BAKED TOMATOES STUFFED WITH PANIR CUBES AND VEGETABLES

*Panir is cheese very widely used in Indian cooking and is a good source of protein for strict vegetarians. It is available at Indian/Pakistani grocers or can be prepared at home (page 140). Serve the stuffed tomatoes on a bed of boiled rice, with a dhal.*

SERVES 4

PREPARATION
*about 30 minutes*
COOKING
*15-20 minutes*

Calories per serving *244*
Total fat *13 g (59%)*
Saturated fat *5 g*
Protein *12 g*
Carbohydrate *23 g*
Cholesterol per serving
*18 mg*
Vitamins *A, B group, C, E*
Minerals *Calcium,
Potassium, Iron, Zinc,
Iodine*

*4 large tomatoes*
*2 oz panir (page 140)*
*2 tablespoons tomato purée*
*1 teaspoon ginger pulp (page 17)*
*1 teaspoon garlic pulp (page 17)*
*1 teaspoon ground coriander*
*1 teaspoon ground cumin*
*salt*
*1 teaspoon chili powder*

*1 tablespoon low-fat sour cream*
*2 tablespoons corn oil*
*4 curry leaves*
*¼ teaspoon mixed onion seeds and mustard seeds*
*2 oz shelled peas*
*½ orange bell pepper, seeded and diced*
*2 oz cauliflower, cut into small florets*
*1 tablespoon chopped fresh cilantro leaves*

**1**  Using a sharp knife, cut the tops off the tomatoes. Using a grapefruit knife, scoop out most of the flesh. Place the hollowed-out tomatoes in a lightly greased ovenproof dish. Preheat the oven to 375°F.

**2**  Cut the panir into ½-inch cubes.

**3**  In a bowl, mix together the tomato purée, ginger, garlic, ground coriander, ground cumin, chili powder, salt to taste, sour cream, and 3 tablespoons water.

**4**  Heat the oil in a kadahi, wok, or deep frying pan and add the curry leaves, and the onion and mustard seeds. Fry for about 20-30 seconds over moderate heat, then add the tomato purée mixture. Stir-fry this for about 3 minutes, until aromatic.

**5**  Add the peas, bell pepper, cauliflower, and cilantro. Cook, stirring, for about 3 minutes, then add the panir cubes. Cook for an additional 2-3 minutes, until the mixture is semi-dry.

**6**  Remove from the heat and spoon the mixture into the tomatoes, then cover with the cut tops. Bake the tomatoes in the oven for 7-10 minutes.

*Baked Tomatoes Stuffed with Panir Cubes and Vegetables*

# BOILED EGG CURRY

SERVES 4

*This creamy egg curry is delicious served with plain boiled rice with saffron.*

PREPARATION
*about 15 minutes*
COOKING
*10-12 minutes,
plus cooking the eggs*

Calories per serving *194*
Total fat *17 g (80%)*
Saturated fat *6 g*
Protein *8 g*
Carbohydrate *2 g*
Cholesterol per serving
*193 mg*
Vitamins *A, B$_2$, B$_3$, B$_{12}$,
Folate, E*
Minerals *Potassium, Iron,
Zinc, Iodine*

**4 hard-boiled eggs**
**2 tablespoons tomato purée**
**1 tablespoon ground coriander**
**large pinch ground cardamom seeds**
**1 teaspoon ginger pulp (page 17)**
**1 teaspoon garlic pulp (page 17)**

**1 tablespoon ground almonds**
**1 tablespoon powdered coconut**
**1 teaspoon chili powder**
**2 tablespoons sunflower oil**
**2 fresh green chilies, chopped**
**2 tablespoons chopped fresh cilantro leaves**

**1** Shell the eggs and cut them in half lengthwise. Arrange the egg halves on a serving platter.
**2** Make a paste in a bowl by combining the tomato purée, ground coriander, cardamom, ginger, garlic, almonds, powdered coconut, and chili powder. Blend together and stir in 1¼ cups water.
**3** Heat the oil in a kadahi, wok, or deep frying pan over moderate heat. Pour in the spice mixture, lower the heat, and cook gently, stirring from time to time, for 5-7 minutes, lowering the heat further if necessary.
**4** Add the fresh chilies and cilantro and cook for an additional 2 minutes. Remove from the heat.
**5** Pour the sauce over the eggs to serve.

# SPICY SPINACH AND POTATO BAKE

SERVES 4

*Spinach is one of my favorite vegetables, and most good supermarkets now sell clean small leaves that can be used in salads or can be lightly blanched or cooked in the way featured here.*

PREPARATION
*about 30 minutes*
COOKING
*15-20 minutes*

Calories per serving *224*
Total fat *10 g (41%)*
Saturated fat *3 g*
Protein *10 g*
Carbohydrate *25 g*
Cholesterol per serving
*10 mg*
Vitamins *A, B group, C, E*
Minerals *Calcium,
Potassium, Iron, Zinc*

**1 lb fresh spinach leaves**
**2 large potatoes**
**salt**
**2 tablespoons sunflower oil**
**1 teaspoon mixed crushed coriander seeds,
mustard seeds, white cumin seeds,
fennel seeds, and onion seeds**
**4 curry leaves**

**1 onion, sliced**
**1 teaspoon chili powder**
**1 teaspoon ginger pulp (page 17)**
**1 teaspoon garlic pulp (page 17)**
**1 medium red bell pepper, seeded and sliced**
**1 tablespoon chopped fresh cilantro leaves**
**2 oz mozzarella cheese, grated**

**1** If necessary, wash the spinach thoroughly and cut off any extra-long stalks. Peel the potatoes and cut into slices.
**2** Blanch the spinach in boiling salted water for about 2 minutes. Drain the water, place the spinach in a sieve to drain any excess water, and set aside.
**3** Preheat the broiler. Heat the sunflower oil in a heavy-bottomed pan, throw in the mixed seeds, and fry over moderate heat for about 30 seconds until aromatic. Add the curry leaves and onion and

fry until the onion is soft and light golden in color.

**4** Reduce heat and add the chili powder, ginger, garlic, and salt to taste. Stir-fry for 30 seconds, then add the potato and stir gently for a minute or so.

**5** Add the bell pepper and spinach, cover with a lid, and cook over low heat for 7-10 minutes until the potato is tender, checking and stirring at least once. Try not to break the potato slices.

**6** Transfer to a heatproof dish and sprinkle with the cilantro and the grated mozzarella cheese. Place under the hot broiler and broil until the cheese has melted and is slightly browned. Serve immediately.

# DOODHI WITH MOONG DHAL

*1 lb doodhi (page 20) or other pumpkin*
*1 cup moong dhal (yellow split mung beans, page 23)*
*1½ tablespoons corn oil*
*½ teaspoon mixed fennel seeds, crushed coriander seeds, and white cumin seeds*
*1 onion, sliced*
*1 teaspoon ginger pulp (page 17)*

*1 teaspoon garlic pulp (page 17)*
*1 teaspoon chili powder*
*salt*
*2 fresh green chilies, slit in the middle*
*2 fresh red chilies, slit in the middle*
*1 tablespoon fresh cilantro leaves, for garnish*

SERVES 4

PREPARATION
*about 20 minutes*
COOKING
*about 35 minutes*

Calories per serving *193*
Total fat *6 g (26%)*
Saturated fat *1 g*
Protein *10 g*
Carbohydrate *28 g*
Cholesterol per serving *None*
Vitamins *A, B₁, B₃, Folate, C, E*
Minerals *Potassium, Iron, Zinc*

**1** Peel the doodhi and cut it into small pieces. Bring about 3¾ cups salted water to a boil and drop in the doodhi. Boil for about 5 minutes. Drain the water and set the doodhi aside.

**2** Wash and pick over the moong dhal for any stones or other debris. Place in a heavy-bottomed pan with water to cover generously. Bring to a boil and cook for about 15 minutes over medium heat, stirring occasionally (a spoon in the pan prevents it boiling over), until soft but not mushy. Drain.

**3** Heat the oil in a large heavy-bottomed pan. Add the mixed seeds and fry for 30 seconds over moderate heat. Add the onion and stir-fry for 3 minutes until softened.

**4** Add the ginger, garlic, chili powder, and salt to taste. Add the lentils and doodhi pieces, and stir gently with a wooden spoon. Drop in the chilies and pour in ⅔ cup water. Lower the heat, cover the pan, and cook for 3-5 minutes.

**5** Serve garnished with the fresh cilantro leaves.

*Overleaf: Doodhi with Moong Dhal, Spicy Spinach and Potato Bake*

# POTATOES IN A SOUR SAUCE

*This curry is traditionally made with lamb and potatoes. However this vegetarian version is equally delicious.*

SERVES 4

PREPARATION
*about 25 minutes*
COOKING
*20-25 minutes*

Calories per serving *469*
Total fat *5 g (10%)*
Saturated fat *1 g*
Protein *13 g*
Carbohydrate *99 g*
Cholesterol per serving
*None*
Vitamins *B₁, B₃, B₆, Folate,*
*C, E*
Minerals *Calcium,*
*Potassium, Iron, Zinc,*
*Selenium, Iodine*

**15 new potatoes**
**1 tablespoon lemon juice**
**1 teaspoon tamarind paste**
**1 teaspoon sugar**
**1½ teaspoons ground coriander**
**½ teaspoon chili powder**
**1 teaspoon garlic pulp (page 17)**
**1 teaspoon ginger pulp (page 17)**

**salt**
**1 tablespoon oil**
**4 curry leaves**
**3 onions, finely chopped**
**1 green bell pepper, seeded and coarsely chopped**
**1 tablespoon chopped fresh mint**
**1 tablespoon chopped fresh cilantro leaves**

**1** Boil the potatoes until soft but not mushy. Drain and, when cool enough to handle, cut in half and set aside.

**2** In a small bowl, blend together the lemon juice, tamarind, sugar, ground coriander, chili powder, garlic, ginger, and salt to taste. Mix to a paste with about 1¼ cups water and set aside.

**3** Heat the oil in a heavy-bottomed saucepan over moderate heat. Add the curry leaves and onions and fry for about 2 minutes, stirring occasionally.

Pour the spice mixture over the top of the onions and cook for 2-3 minutes, stirring occasionally, until aromatic and the onions are softened.

**4** Add the potatoes, mixing them in gently. Cover and cook for an additional 5-7 minutes, until the potatoes are tender. Remove the lid and stir gently. The sauce should be quite thick by this time.

**5** Stir in the bell pepper, mint, and cilantro, and serve hot.

# CHANA DHAL WITH PANIR AND TOMATOES

*Tomatoes and panir make this crunchy dhal visually very attractive. It is delicious served simply, with just an accompaniment of plain boiled rice.*

SERVES 4

PREPARATION
*about 15 minutes*
COOKING
*about 20 minutes*

**6 oz chana dhal (page 23)**
**1 onion, diced**
**1 teaspoon garam masala**
**1 teaspoon garlic pulp (page 17)**
**1 teaspoon ginger pulp (page 17)**
**½ teaspoon chili powder**
**½ teaspoon mango powder**
**salt**
**chopped fresh cilantro leaves, for garnish**

**for the tarka (seasoned oil):**
**1 tablespoon corn oil**
**½ teaspoon white cumin seeds**
**4 curry leaves**
**3 whole garlic cloves**
**6 pearl onions, peeled**
**6 bite-sized cubes panir (page 140)**
**6 cherry tomatoes**

1 Wash and pick over the chana dhal or split peas, discarding any stones or other debris. Place in a heavy-bottomed saucepan with the onion, garam masala, garlic, ginger, chili powder, mango powder, salt to taste, and about 2½ cups water. Bring to a boil and cook for about 15 minutes over medium heat, stirring occasionally (put a spoon in the pan to prevent it from boiling over).

2 Meanwhile, to prepare the tarka, heat the oil over moderate heat. Add the cumin seeds, curry leaves, garlic cloves, pearl onions, panir cubes, and cherry tomatoes, and fry for 1 or 2 minutes, until aromatic, shaking the pan continuously to prevent the whole spices from burning.

3 Once the dhal is cooked and the water is almost entirely absorbed, pour the tarka over the lentils and mix well.

4 Serve sprinkled with the chopped cilantro.

Calories per serving *274*
Total fat *7 g (23%)*
Saturated fat *2 g*
Protein *15 g*
Carbohydrate *41 g*
Cholesterol per serving *15 mg*
Vitamins *A, B group, C, E*
Minerals *Calcium, Potassium, Iron, Zinc, Iodine*

# CAULIFLOWER WITH PEPPERS

*Try to choose small cauliflowers, even if it means you need to buy two, as these are not only usually fresher-looking but also firmer and easier to manage. This very colorful vegetarian curry is best eaten with freshly made chapatis.*

**2 small cauliflowers (or 1 medium, see above)**
**8 new potatoes**
**1 red bell pepper**
**1 yellow bell pepper**
**2 oz shelled peas**
**1 tablespoon corn oil**
**¼ teaspoon white cumin seeds**
**6 curry leaves**
**3 whole dried red chilies**
**2 onions, sliced**
**3 garlic cloves, chopped**
**2 teaspoons shredded ginger**
**1 teaspoon chili powder**
**¼ teaspoon turmeric**
**salt**
**1 tablespoon chopped fresh cilantro leaves, for garnish**

SERVES 4

PREPARATION
*about 20 minutes*
COOKING
*12-15 minutes*

1 Cut the cauliflower into small florets; cut the potatoes into slices; seed the peppers and cut into strips. Thaw the peas if frozen. Set aside.

2 Pour the oil into a heavy-bottomed saucepan over moderate heat and add the cumin seeds, curry leaves, and whole red chilies. Quickly move them around to prevent burning.

3 Add the sliced onions, chopped garlic, and shredded ginger, and cook for about 2 minutes, stirring to prevent the onions from burning.

4 Add all the prepared vegetables, followed by the chili powder, turmeric, and salt to taste. Blend everything together and cover with a lid. Lower the heat and cook for 5-7 minutes. The steam should cook the vegetables; if the mixture is getting too dry, add about ⅔ cup water.

5 Served garnished with the cilantro.

Calories per serving *185*
Total fat *4 g (22%)*
Saturated fat *1 g*
Protein *8 g*
Carbohydrate *30 g*
Cholesterol per serving *None*
Vitamins *A, B₁, B₃, B₆, Folate, C, E*
Minerals *Potassium, Iron, Zinc*

# CORN AND PEAS WITH PANIR

SERVES 4

*This quick stir-fry makes a good side dish, or even a main course served with freshly made chapatis.*

PREPARATION
*about 10 minutes*
COOKING
*12-15 minutes*

Calories per serving *145*
Total fat *5 g (28%)*
Saturated fat *1 g*
Protein *5 g*
Carbohydrate *23 g*
Cholesterol per serving
*None*
Vitamins A, B₁, B₃, B₆,
*Folate, C, E*
Minerals *Potassium, Iron,
Zinc*

**1 large carrot**
**½ red bell pepper**
**1 tablespoon corn oil**
**2 onions, finely chopped**
**8 oz corn kernels**
**4½ oz shelled peas**
**1-inch piece ginger, grated**

**2 garlic cloves, finely chopped**
**1½ teaspoons crushed dried red chilies**
**salt**
**10-12 cubes panir (page 140)**
**fresh mint leaves, for garnish**
**sprigs of cilantro, for garnish**

**1** Chop the carrot. Seed and dice the red bell pepper.

**2** Heat the oil over moderate heat. Add the chopped onions and fry for 2-3 minutes, stirring occasionally. Add the corn, peas, chopped carrot, and bell pepper, followed by the ginger, garlic, crushed chilies, and salt to taste. Continue to stir-fry over moderate heat for 3-5 minutes.

**3** Add the cubes of panir and cook for an additional 3-5 minutes.

**4** Serve garnished with the mint and cilantro.

# BAY RICE WITH PEAS

SERVES 4

*Rice and peas are always a good combination. This dish is delicately flavored with ginger, garlic, bay leaf, and some other whole spices.*

PREPARATION
*about 10 minutes*
COOKING
*20-25 minutes,
plus 5 minutes
standing*

Calories per serving *268*
Total fat *5 g (28%)*
Saturated fat *1 g*
Protein *6 g*
Carbohydrate *52 g*
Cholesterol per serving
*None*
Vitamins B₃, *Folate, E*
Minerals *Iron, Potassium*

**2 cups basmati rice**
**1 tablespoon each olive and corn oil**
**1 onion, sliced**
**1 teaspoon ginger pulp (page 17)**
**1 teaspoon garlic pulp (page 17)**
**salt**

**1 bay leaf**
**3 whole cloves**
**1 small piece cinnamon stick**
**6-8 black peppercorns**
**2 whole black cardamom pods**
**3 oz shelled peas**

**1** Wash the rice well and leave to soak.

**2** Heat the oils in a heavy-bottomed saucepan. Add the onion and fry over moderate heat until golden. Add the ginger, garlic, salt to taste, bay leaf, cloves, cinnamon, peppercorns, and cardamom. Cook for about 30 seconds until aromatic.

**3** Drain the rice and add to the oil, stirring gently so you do not damage it. Add the peas. Pour in 3 cups water and bring to a boil. Lower the heat, cover the pan, and cook for 10-15 minutes until the water is absorbed and the rice is cooked.

**4** Let the rice rest off the heat, covered, for 5 minutes before serving. If you prefer, remove the cinnamon and cloves before serving.

*Corn and Peas with Panir*

# SPINACH WITH GARLIC AND FROMAGE BLANC

SERVES 4

PREPARATION
*about 15 minutes*
COOKING
*10-15 minutes*

Calories per serving *87*
Total fat *5 g (52%)*
Saturated fat *1 g*
Protein *6 g*
Carbohydrate *4 g*
Cholesterol per serving
*3 mg*
Vitamins *A, B group, C, E*
Minerals *Calcium,*
*Potassium, Iron, Zinc*

*1½ lbs fresh spinach leaves, chopped*
*salt*
*1 tablespoon olive oil*
*1-inch piece cinnamon stick*
*2 whole cloves*

*3 garlic cloves, coarsely chopped*
*2 fresh red chilies, chopped*
*2 tablespoons chopped fresh cilantro leaves*
*2 tablespoons low-fat fromage blanc*

1  Wash the spinach thoroughly, unless it is ready prepared, and blanch it in boiling salted water for 2 minutes. Drain the spinach well and set aside.
2  Heat the olive oil in a kadahi, wok, or deep frying pan over low heat. Add the cinnamon, cloves, garlic, 1 of the chopped chilies, and the spinach.

Quickly stir-fry over moderate heat until wilted.
3  Add salt to taste, the cilantro, and the remaining red chili, and continue to stir-fry over low heat for an additional 2-3 minutes.
4  Stir in the fromage blanc and cook for an additional 1-1½ minutes.

# SPICY RICE AND VEGETABLE STIR-FRY

SERVES 4

PREPARATION
*about 20 minutes*
COOKING
*30-35 minutes,*
*plus 5 minutes*
*standing*

Calories per serving *338*
Total fat *7 g (19%)*
Saturated fat *1 g*
Protein *8 g*
Carbohydrate *61 g*
Cholesterol per serving
*None*
Vitamins *A, B₁, B₃, B₆,*
*Folate, C, E*
Minerals *Potassium, Iron*

*2 cups basmati rice*
*2 tablespoons corn oil*
*6 curry leaves*
*½ teaspoon mixed onion seeds, mustard seeds,*
*cumin seeds, and fenugreek seeds*
*1 teaspoon garlic pulp (page 17)*
*1 teaspoon ginger pulp (page 17)*
*1 onion, chopped*
*2 tomatoes, sliced*

*2 oz corn kernels*
*2 oz shelled peas*
*2 oz green beans, cut into pieces*
*1 carrot, diced*
*2 tablespoons lemon juice*
*2 tablespoons chopped fresh cilantro leaves*
*2 fresh green chilies, diced*
*salt*

1  Wash the rice until the water runs clear and leave to soak while you prepare the vegetables.
2  Heat the oil in a large heavy-bottomed saucepan. Add the curry leaves and the mixed seeds and fry for about 45 seconds over moderate heat until aromatic. Lower the heat, add the garlic, ginger, and onion. Stir-fry for about 3 minutes.
3  Add the other vegetables, beginning with the

tomatoes, and stir-fry each for about 2 minutes.
4  Add the lemon juice, cilantro, chilies, and salt to taste. Drain rice well, add it to the vegetables, and stir-fry for an additional minute. Add 3 cups water and bring to a boil. Reduce the heat to medium-low, cover and cook for 10-15 minutes, until all the water is absorbed and the rice is cooked. Let stand, covered, for 5 minutes off the heat before serving.

*Spinach with Garlic and Fromage Blanc*

# Bread and Rice

# NAAN
## *Yeasted Bread*

*There are many ways of making naan, but this recipe is one of the simplest. Naan should be served warm, preferably as soon as they are cooked. If you aren't concerned about calories and fat, and want a more authentic naan, use butter rather than olive oil.*

MAKES 6

PREPARATION
*about 25 minutes, plus 3-4 hours rising*
COOKING
*15-20 minutes*

Calories per serving *350*
Total fat *19 g (44%)*
Saturated fat *11 g*
Protein *6 g*
Carbohydrate *50 g*
Cholesterol per serving *11 mg*
Vitamins *A, B₁, B₃, B₆, Folate*
Minerals *Calcium, Iron, Iodine, Potassium*

**1 teaspoon sugar**
**1 teaspoon compressed fresh yeast**
**⅔ cup warm water**
**2 cups all-purpose flour, plus more for dusting**
**1 tablespoon ghee or melted butter**

**1 teaspoon salt**
**¼ cup olive oil**
**1 teaspoon sesame seeds or poppy seeds**
**corn oil, for brushing the grill pan**

**1** Put the sugar and the yeast in a cup with the warm water. Mix well until the yeast has dissolved and leave for 10 minutes or until frothy.

**2** Place the flour in a large mixing bowl. Make a well in the middle, add the ghee or butter and the salt, and pour in the yeast mixture. Mix well, using your hands and adding a little more water if required to achieve a soft and pliable dough.

**3** Turn the dough out on a floured surface and knead for about 5 minutes or until smooth.

**4** Place the dough back in the bowl, cover, and leave to rise in a warm place for 3-4 hours, until doubled in size.

**5** Preheat the broiler and line the broiler pan with foil. Grease the foil lightly with corn oil.

**6** Turn the dough out on a floured surface and knead it for an additional 2 minutes. Break it into 6 balls with your hand and pat these into rounds about 5 inches in diameter and ½ inch thick.

**7** Place 2 or 3 rounds in the broiler pan, brush with some of the olive oil, and sprinkle with sesame or poppy seeds. Broil for 7-10 minutes, turning twice, brushing with oil and sprinkling with sesame or poppy seeds each time, until golden and lightly puffed. Wrap in foil to keep warm while you cook the rest.

**8** Serve warm as soon as all are cooked.

# CHAPATI
## *Unleavened Bread*

*This is one of the healthiest of Indian breads, because it contains no fat. However, some people like to brush it with a little melted butter before serving. Ideally chapatis should be eaten as they come off the* thawa *(a slightly concave circular cast-iron plate or skillet) or out of the frying pan; if that is not practical, however, keep them warm after cooking by wrapping them in foil. In India, chapatis are sometimes cooked on a naked flame, which makes them puff up. Allow about 2 per person.*

*Previous pages: Chapati and Naan*

**2 cups whole-wheat chapati flour (page 28), plus more, for dusting**

**½ teaspoon salt**

1  Place the flour in a mixing bowl with the salt. Make a well in the middle of the flour and gradually stir in ¾ cup water, mixing well with your fingers to form a supple dough.

2  Knead the dough for 7-10 minutes, until it is soft and pliable. Ideally, leave it to rest for 15-20 minutes; if time is short, roll it out immediately.

3  Divide the dough into 8-12 roughly equal portions. Roll out each piece on a well-floured surface. Have some foil ready in which to wrap the cooked chapatis to keep them warm.

4  Place a heavy-bottomed frying pan or a thawa over high heat. When it is almost smoking hot, lower the heat to moderate. Place a chapati in the pan and, when it bubbles, turn it over. Press it down with a clean dish towel or a spatula and turn again when small patches of brown start to appear on the underside and it begins to puff up.

5  Remove from the pan and keep warm. Repeat the process until all the chapatis are cooked.

PREPARATION
*15-20 minutes, plus 15-20 minutes standing (optional)*
COOKING
*30-40 minutes*

Calories per serving *208*
Total fat *1 g (3%)*
Saturated fat *None*
Protein *7 g*
Carbohydrate *46 g*
Cholesterol per serving *None*
Vitamins *B₁, B₃*
Minerals *Potassium, Iron, Zinc*

# ROTI
## *Gram Flour Bread*

**1 cup whole-wheat flour, plus more for dusting**
**1 cup gram flour (page 29)**
**1 tablespoon chopped fresh cilantro leaves**
**1 fresh red chili, seeded and chopped**

**1 small onion, finely diced**
**¼ teaspoon onion seeds**
**large pinch salt**
**3-4 tablespoons corn oil**

1  Sift both the flours into a mixing bowl. Add the cilantro, chili, onion, onion seeds, and salt. Using a fork, blend everything together. Gradually pour in about ¾ cup water, just enough to form a soft pliable dough. Knead the dough on a floured surface for about 45 seconds, then set aside for 5-7 minutes to rest.

2  Divide the dough into 8-10 balls and, on a well-floured surface, roll each into a 5-6-inch round.

3  Heat a thawa or a nonstick frying pan over a high heat and, when the pan is very hot, turn the heat down slightly. Place one of the dough rounds on the pan and, after about 30 seconds, sprinkle 1 teaspoon of oil over it and turn it over. Cook, moving the roti around on the pan, and turn it over again. The roti will puff up, so press it down with a spatula to ensure even cooking. When the roti is well browned on both sides, remove and keep warm, wrapped in foil, while you cook the remaining roti in the same way.

PREPARATION
*about 20 minutes, plus 5-7 minutes resting*
COOKING
*15-20 minutes*

Calories per serving *112*
Total fat *5 g (40%)*
Saturated fat *1 g*
Protein *4 g*
Carbohydrate *14 g*
Cholesterol per serving *None*
Vitamins *B₁, B₃, B₆, Folate, E*
Minerals *Potassium, Iron, Zinc, Selenium*

# AROMATIC RICE WITH PEAS

SERVES 4

*I have made boiled rice more interesting by adding some whole spices and peas.*

PREPARATION
*5 minutes*
COOKING
*15-20 minutes,
plus 5 minutes
standing*

Calories per serving *238*
Total fat *1 g (2%)*
Saturated fat *None*
Protein *6 g*
Carbohydrate *52 g*
Cholesterol per serving
*None*
Vitamins *B₃, Folate*
Minerals *Potassium, Iron*

| | |
|---|---|
| **2 cups basmati rice** | **1 fresh bay leaf** |
| **2 cardamom pods** | **½ teaspoon salt** |
| **¼ teaspoon black cumin seeds** | **3 oz shelled peas** |
| **1 cinnamon stick** | **fried sliced onions, for garnish (optional)** |
| **4 black peppercorns** | |

**1** Wash the rice until the water runs clear and leave to soak in fresh water.

**2** Pour 3 cups water into a large saucepan and add the whole spices, followed by the salt. Place the saucepan over high heat and when the water begins to boil, lower the heat. Drain the rice and add it to the water with the peas. Cover with a lid and cook over medium heat for 10-15 minutes, until all the water has been absorbed and the rice is cooked.

**3** Let the rice stand off the heat, covered, for 5 minutes. Serve with a slotted spoon to prevent the rice from becoming mushy. Garnish with fried onions if you like.

# TAMATAR AUR MATAR KAY CHAWAL
## *Tomato and Pea Rice*

SERVES 4

PREPARATION
*about 10 minutes*
COOKING
*30-35 minutes*

Calories per serving *282*
Total fat *4 g (11%)*
Saturated fat *1 g*
Protein *6 g*
Carbohydrate *56 g*
Cholesterol per serving
*None*
Vitamins *B₁, Folate, C, E*
Minerals *Potassium, Iron*

| | |
|---|---|
| **2 cups basmati rice** | **½ teaspoon ginger pulp (page 17)** |
| **2 tablespoons corn oil** | **½ teaspoon garlic pulp (page 17)** |
| **1 medium onion, sliced** | **2 tomatoes, sliced** |
| **large pinch onion seeds** | **salt** |
| **6-8 curry leaves** | **2 oz shelled peas** |

**1** Wash the rice until the water runs clear. Leave it to soak in fresh water while you do the rest of the preparation.

**2** Heat the oil in a large heavy-bottomed saucepan over moderate heat. Add the onion, onion seeds, and curry leaves, and fry for about 5 minutes, stirring frequently, until the onion is soft and golden.

**3** Add the ginger, garlic, tomato, and salt to taste. Stir-fry for another 3 minutes.

**4** Drain the rice and add to the pan, stirring gently for about 1 minute, then add 3 cups water and the peas. Bring to a boil, then lower the heat, cover the pan tightly, and simmer gently for about 10-15 minutes, until all the water is absorbed and the rice is tender.

*Aromatic Rice with Peas*

# RICE WITH PINE NUTS

*This is an excellent and versatile rice dish. I especially enjoy it with Lemon and Garlic Fish (page 49).*

SERVES 4

PREPARATION
*10 minutes*
COOKING
*20-25 minutes,
plus 5 minutes
standing*

Calories per serving *306*
Total fat *9 g (26%)*
Saturated fat *1 g*
Protein *6 g*
Carbohydrate *51 g*
Cholesterol per serving
*None*
Vitamins *B₃, E*
Minerals *Potassium, Iron*

**2 cups basmati rice**
**1 tablespoon corn oil**
**¼ teaspoon mustard seeds**
**4 curry leaves**
**½ teaspoon ginger pulp (page 17)**
**½ teaspoon garlic pulp (page 17)**
**½ teaspoon salt**
**2 tablespoons pine nuts**

1  Wash the rice until the water runs clear. Leave to soak in fresh water.

2  Heat the oil in a large heavy-bottomed saucepan. Add the mustard seeds and curry leaves and fry for about 40 seconds until aromatic. Lower the heat and add the ginger, garlic, salt, and pine nuts. Stir-fry for an additional 30 seconds.

3  Drain the water from the rice and pour the rice into the pan. Continue to stir-fry for another 30 seconds, then pour in 3 cups water. Bring to a boil, then reduce the heat to moderate. Cover the pan and cook for about 10-15 minutes, until all the water is absorbed and the rice is cooked.

4  Let the rice stand off the heat, covered, for 5-7 minutes before serving.

# RICE WITH DESICCATED COCONUT

SERVES 4

PREPARATION
*about 20 minutes*
COOKING
*24-30 minutes,
plus 5 minutes
standing*

Calories per serving *322*
Total fat *8 g (22%)*
Saturated fat *4 g*
Protein *6 g*
Carbohydrate *56 g*
Cholesterol per serving
*None*
Vitamins *A, B₃, B₆, C, E*
Minerals *Potassium, Iron*

**2 cups basmati rice**
**1 tablespoon corn oil**
**4-6 curry leaves**
**large pinch onion seeds**
**1 medium onion, sliced**
**2 garlic cloves, sliced**
**1 teaspoon shredded ginger**
**salt**
**1 large carrot, diced**
**2 tablespoons desiccated coconut**
**1 tablespoon chopped fresh cilantro leaves**
**1 fresh red chili, chopped**

1  Wash the basmati rice until the water runs clear, about 3 washes. Leave to soak in fresh water.

2  Meanwhile, in a large heavy-bottomed saucepan heat the oil over moderate heat. Add the curry leaves, onion seeds, and onion, and stir-fry for about 2 minutes until aromatic.

3  Add the garlic, ginger, salt to taste, carrots, half the coconut, and half the cilantro. Mix well.

4  Drain the rice and add it to the onion mixture. Stir-fry gently for about 1 minute.

5  Add the remaining coconut, cilantro, and the chopped chili, followed by 3 cups water. Bring to a boil, lower the heat to moderate, cover, and cook for 15-20 minutes, until the rice is just tender.

6  Let the rice stand off the heat, covered, for about 5 minutes before serving.

# SAFFRON RICE MOLDS

*2 cups basmati rice*
*1 tablespoon olive oil*
*1 tablespoon corn oil, plus more for the molds*
*2 black cardamom pods*
*large pinch black cumin seeds*
*6 black peppercorns*

*2 cloves*
*salt*
*½ teaspoon saffron threads*
*2 tablespoons golden raisins*
*1 tablespoon sliced almonds*

SERVES 4

PREPARATION
*10 minutes*
COOKING
*about 30 minutes,*
*plus 5-7 minutes*
*standing*

Calories per serving *295*
Total fat *8 g (25%)*
Saturated fat *1 g*
Protein *5 g*
Carbohydrate *50 g*
Cholesterol per serving
*None*
Vitamins *E*
Minerals *Potassium, Iron*

**1** Rinse the basmati rice thoroughly until the water runs clear. Leave it to soak in fresh water while preparing the rest of the ingredients.

**2** In a large heavy-bottomed saucepan, heat the oils together over moderate heat for about 30 seconds, then add the cardamom pods, cumin seeds, peppercorns, cloves, and salt to taste. Lower the heat and stir.

**3** Drain the rice, add to the pan, and stir gently. Add the saffron, raisins, almonds, and 3 cups water.

Bring to a boil, lower the heat, cover, and cook for about 10-15 minutes, until the water is fully absorbed and the rice is tender. Let stand, off the heat, still covered, for 5-7 minutes.

**4** While the rice is cooking, preheat the oven to 375°F and lightly grease 4 ramekins with corn oil. Press the rice into them and warm through in the oven for about 5-10 minutes.

**5** Carefully unmold the rice to serve.

# Salads, Side Dishes, and Accompaniments

# TOMATO AND ONION SALAD

SERVES 4

PREPARATION
*about 15 minutes*

Calories per serving *39*
Total fat *1 g (9%)*
Saturated fat *None*
Protein *1 g*
Carbohydrate *8 g*
Cholesterol per serving
*None*
Vitamins *A, B₁, B₃, B₆,*
*Folate, C, E*
Minerals *Potassium*

*Versions of this versatile fresh-tasting salad are served at most dinner tables in India and Pakistan.*

**1 red onion, diced**
**2 tomatoes, diced**
**1 large carrot, diced**
**½ medium cucumber, diced**
**1 fresh green chili, seeded and sliced**

**1 tablespoon chopped fresh cilantro leaves**
**1 tablespoon chopped fresh mint, plus extra sprigs for garnish (optional)**
**salt**
**2 tablespoons lime juice**

**1**  Put the diced onion, tomatoes, carrot, and cucumber in a salad bowl. Add the chili, herbs, and salt to taste.

**2**  Using a fork, gently mix everything together.

**3**  Sprinkle on the lime juice and garnish with sprigs of mint to serve if you wish.

# BOMBAY POTATOES

SERVES 4

PREPARATION
*about 15 minutes*
COOKING
*15-20 minutes*

Calories per serving *222*
Total fat *4 g (27%)*
Saturated fat *1 g*
Protein *4 g*
Carbohydrate
*39 g*
Cholesterol per serving
*None*
Vitamins *B₁, B₃, B₆,*
*Folate, C, E*
Minerals *Potassium, Iron,*
*Iodine*

*Bombay potatoes get their sweet-and-sour flavor from sugar and tamarind paste and make a delicious accompaniment to almost any meal.*

**15 new potatoes, scrubbed and halved**
**salt**
**2 tablespoons tomato purée**
**2 tablespoons tomato ketchup**
**1 tablespoon tamarind paste**
**1 teaspoon sugar**
**1 teaspoon ginger pulp (page 17)**
**1½ teaspoons ground coriander**

**1 teaspoon garlic pulp (page 17)**
**1 teaspoon chili powder**
**1 tablespoon lemon juice**
**2 tablespoons corn oil**
**¼ teaspoon onion seeds**
**6 curry leaves**
**1 tablespoon chopped fresh cilantro leaves**
**1 large fresh green chili, chopped**

**1**  Cook the new potatoes in boiling salted water until just tender. Drain and set aside.

**2**  Meanwhile, in a small bowl, combine the tomato purée, ketchup, tamarind paste, sugar, ginger, ground coriander, garlic, chili powder, lemon juice, and salt to taste, and 1 cup water.

**3**  In a heavy-bottomed saucepan over moderate heat, heat the oil with the onion seeds and curry leaves. Lower the heat and add the tomato paste. Quickly stir-fry for about 1 minute, then add the potatoes. Continue to stir-fry for an additional 2 minutes.

**4**  Stir in the cilantro and chilies and serve.

*Previous pages: Bombay Potatoes, Mango and Apple Chutney (page 139) and Tomato and Onion Salad*

# MIXED SALAD WITH CORN

*Although not traditional, this salad, with its garlic-flavored dressing, has a nice, slightly spicy tang.*

*3 whole radicchio leaves*
*6 whole iceberg lettuce leaves*
*1 celery stalk, sliced*
*1 scallion, chopped*
*½ cucumber, sliced*
*1 medium-sized cooked beet, diced*
*2 oz fresh cooked or thawed frozen corn kernels*
*2 oz shelled fresh baby peas*
*6 cherry tomatoes (preferably with their stalks)*

*for the dressing:*
*1 tablespoon olive oil*
*½ teaspoon crushed dried red chilies*
*1 tablespoon lemon juice*
*2 garlic cloves, crushed*
*1 teaspoon superfine sugar*
*¼ teaspoon freshly ground black pepper*
*salt*
*1 tablespoon chopped fresh cilantro*

**1**  Line a salad bowl with the radicchio and iceberg lettuce leaves. Sprinkle the celery, scallion, and cucumber over the top. Make a circle around the edge with the diced beet.

**2**  Mix together the corn and peas and arrange them in the center of the salad. Arrange the cherry tomatoes all around the edge of the salad.

**3**  To make the dressing, place the olive oil in a small bowl with the dried red chilies, lemon juice, crushed garlic, sugar, black pepper, salt to taste, and cilantro. Mix well with a spoon and pour all over the salad to serve.

SERVES 4

PREPARATION
*about 20 minutes*

Calories per serving *77*
Total fat *3 g (41%)*
Saturated fat *1 g*
Protein *3 g*
Carbohydrate *9 g*
Cholesterol per serving *None*
Vitamins *B₁, B₃, B₆, Folate, C, E*
Minerals *Potassium, Iron*

# SPICY POTATO AND KIDNEY BEAN SALAD

*6-8 new potatoes*
*salt*
*¼ cup low-fat plain yogurt*
*1¼ cups low-fat fromage blanc*
*1 garlic clove, finely chopped*
*1 teaspoon crushed dried red chilies*
*1 teaspoon sugar*

*1 tablespoon lime juice*
*2 tablespoons chopped fresh cilantro leaves*
*½ red bell pepper, seeded and diced*
*1 tablespoon chopped fresh mint*
*¼ cup canned red kidney beans, drained*
*1 scallion, chopped, for garnish*

**1**  Scrub and halve the potatoes, then boil in salted water until soft but not mushy. Remove from the heat and leave in the water, covered.

**2**  In a bowl, whisk together the yogurt, fromage blanc, and garlic. Gradually add the crushed red chilies, sugar, lime juice, cilantro, and salt to taste.

Mix everything together well and set aside.

**3**  Drain the potatoes and add them to the yogurt sauce, followed by the bell pepper, mint, and beans. Mix together well.

**4**  Transfer to a serving dish and serve garnished with the chopped scallion.

SERVES 4

PREPARATION
*about 20 minutes*
COOKING
*about 15 minutes*

Calories per serving *130*
Total fat *6 g (7%)*
Saturated fat *1 g*
Protein *6 g*
Carbohydrate *26 g*
Cholesterol per serving *2 mg*
Vitamins *A, B group, C*
Minerals *Calcium, Potassium, Iron, Zinc, Iodine*

# CHICKPEA SALAD

SERVES 4

PREPARATION
*about 20 minutes*
COOKING
*2-3 minutes*

Calories per serving *187*
Total fat *7 g (32%)*
Saturated fat *1 g*
Protein *10 g*
Carbohydrate *24 g*
Cholesterol per serving
*None*
Vitamins *A, B₁, B₃, B₆,*
*Folate, C, E*
Minerals *Calcium,*
*Potassium, Iron, Zinc,*
*Iodine*

*1¾ cups canned chickpeas*
*1 teaspoon cumin seeds*
*1 teaspoon coriander seeds*
*½ red bell pepper, seeded and diced*
*½ orange bell pepper, seeded and diced*
*¼ small red cabbage, shredded*
*1 iceberg lettuce, shredded*
*1 large carrot, diced*
*½ cucumber, sliced*
*½ red onion, sliced*

*1 teaspoon chopped fresh cilantro (optional)*
*1 teaspoon chopped fresh mint (optional)*

*for the dressing:*
*2 garlic cloves, crushed*
*salt*
*1 tablespoon olive oil*
*2 tablespoons lemon juice*
*large pinch sugar*
*1 teaspoon crushed dried red chilies*

**1** Drain the chickpeas. Toast the cumin and coriander seeds in a nonstick pan until fragrant (about 1 minute), then crush them roughly with a mortar and pestle.

**2** To make the dressing, in a small bowl, combine all of the ingredients and set aside.

**3** Mix the remaining salad ingredients in a salad bowl. Pour the dressing over the top and toss to coat uniformly.

**4** Sprinkle the cumin and coriander seeds over the top before serving.

*Chickpea Salad*

# SPINACH AND SWEET POTATO SALAD

*This very colorful salad, which features sweet potato, spinach, carrots, and red and green bell peppers, is served with a crunchy nut dressing.*

SERVES 4

PREPARATION
*about 20 minutes*
COOKING
*about 25 minutes*

Calories per serving *410*
Total fat *26 g (58%)*
Saturated fat *1 g*
Protein *17 g*
Carbohydrate *28 g*
Cholesterol per serving
*4 mg*
Vitamins *A, B group, C, E*
Minerals *Calcium,
Potassium, Iron, Zinc,
Iodine*

**1 medium-sized sweet potato**
**salt**
**1 large carrot, sliced**
**20-25 baby spinach leaves**
**1 red bell pepper, seeded and sliced**
**½ green bell pepper, seeded and diced**
**2 scallions, sliced at an angle**

**for the dressing:**
**2 tablespoons pine nuts**
**2 tablespoons golden raisins**
**5 walnuts**
**1 tablespoon chopped fresh cilantro leaves**
**1 fresh red chili, finely chopped**
**1 tablespoon honey**
**1 tablespoon low-fat plain yogurt**
**2 tablespoons low-fat fromage blanc**
**salt**
**coarsely ground black pepper**

**1**  Cook the sweet potato in boiling salted water until soft. Drain and slice, then set aside. Boil the carrot slices in the same way, drain, and let cool.

**2**  On a serving plate, mix the spinach leaves, sweet potato, and carrot slices. Decorate with the red and green bell peppers and chopped scallions.

**3**  To make the dressing, in a small bowl, mix together the pine nuts, golden raisins, and walnuts

(if you like, reserve a little of each and some of the chili for garnish). In another bowl, mix together the cilantro, chili, honey, yogurt, fromage blanc, and salt to taste. Pour this over the nuts and raisins and blend everything together. Season with coarsely ground black pepper.

**4**  Serve the dressing with the salad, garnished with the reserved chili, nuts, and fruit if you wish.

*Spinach and Sweet Potato Salad*

# KACHOOMER WITH BLACK-EYED PEAS

*Kachoomer is a popular accompaniment to Indian and Pakistani meals. It is usually made with just tomatoes, onion, cilantro, and chilies, I like to embellish it with a few more ingredients.*

SERVES 4

PREPARATION
*about 25 minutes*
COOKING
*about 10 minutes*

Calories per serving *39*
Total fat *1 g (9%)*
Saturated fat *None*
Protein *2 g*
Carbohydrate *7 g*
Cholesterol per serving
*None*
Vitamins *B₁, B₃, B₆,*
*Folate, C*
Minerals *Potassium, Iron*

*2 tablespoons black-eyed peas (soaked overnight if possible)*
*1 red onion, finely chopped*
*½ cucumber, diced*
*2 tomatoes, sliced*
*2 fresh green chilies, chopped*
*1 large carrot, finely grated*

*1 tablespoon chopped fresh mint*
*2 tablespoons chopped fresh cilantro leaves*
*1 garlic clove, finely chopped*
*2 tablespoons lemon juice*
*½ teaspoon coarsely ground black peppercorns*
*salt*
*mint sprigs, for garnish*

**1**  Boil the black-eyed peas in salted water for about 10 minutes until just tender, drain the water, and set aside.

**2**  Place all the vegetables and herbs in a serving dish with the drained black-eyed peas. Using a fork, gently mix everything together, trying not to mash any of the vegetables.

**3**  Mix in the garlic, lemon juice, black pepper, and salt to taste.

**4**  Serve garnished with the mint sprigs.

# MANGO AND APPLE CHUTNEY

*Chutneys and pickles are served at most Indian and Pakistani meals. Usually each diner takes about 1 teaspoon of chutney and puts it on the side of his or her plate.*

**2 large mangoes**
**2 large green cooking apples**
**2 whole cloves**
**1½-inch piece cinnamon stick**
**1 teaspoon crushed dried red chilies**
**6 tablespoons brown sugar**

**1 teaspoon garam masala**
**1 teaspoon shredded ginger**
**1 teaspoon salt**
**1¼ cups malt vinegar**
**1 tablespoon chopped fresh mint**

**1**  Peel the mangoes, remove and discard the pits, then chop the flesh coarsely (page 24). Peel and core the apples, then slice them coarsely. Place both fruits in a heavy-bottomed saucepan.

**2**  Add the cloves, cinnamon, crushed red chilies, brown sugar, garam masala, shredded ginger, salt, and malt vinegar. Stir everything together, bring to a simmer and cook over medium heat for 10-15 minutes, until most of the liquid has evaporated.

**3**  Stir in the mint and cook for an additional 2 minutes. Leave to cool.

**4**  Transfer to a sterile jar and seal. This chutney will keep in the refrigerator for up to 1 month.

PREPARATION
*about 10 minutes*
COOKING
*15-20 minutes, plus cooling*

Calories per serving *180*
Total fat *1 g (2%)*
Saturated fat *None*
Protein *1 g*
Carbohydrate *43 g*
Cholesterol per serving *None*
Vitamins A, *B₃, B₆, Folate, C, E*
Minerals *Potassium, Iron*

# SWEET-AND-SOUR CHICKPEA AND SESAME SEED CHUTNEY

**½ cup drained canned chickpeas**
**½ cup sesame seeds**
**2 tablespoons sugar**
**1 tablespoon tamarind pulp**
**2 green chilies, coarsely chopped**

**2 tablespoons chopped cilantro**
**salt**
**4 scallions, chopped, for garnish**
**1 red chili, sliced, for garnish**

**1**  In a food processor, grind the chickpeas to a smooth paste. Transfer to a mixing bowl.

**2**  Roast the sesame seeds in a dry frying pan for about 1 minute over a moderate heat, moving the pan constantly to toss the seeds around and prevent them burning. Allow to cool briefly, then grind to a powder in a food processor.

**3**  Add the ground sesame seeds to the chickpeas, followed by the sugar, tamarind, green chilies, half the chopped cilantro, and salt to taste. Process this mixture in the food processor briefly, in batches if necessary, until everything is well mixed.

**4**  Transfer to a serving bowl and garnish with the remaining cilantro, chopped scallions, and red chili.

PREPARATION
*about 25 minutes*
COOKING
*2-3 minutes*

Calories per serving *204*
Total fat *13 g (58%)*
Saturated fat *2 g*
Protein *7 g*
Carbohydrate *16 g*
Cholesterol per serving *None*
Vitamins *B₁, B₆, Folate, C, E*
Minerals *Calcium, Potassium, Iron, Zinc*

# DATE AND TAMARIND CHUTNEY

PREPARATION
*about 10 minutes*

*This chutney is easy to make and adds a sweet-and-sour flavor to any meal. Pitted and chopped dates are usually available at most supermarkets.*

Calories per serving *143*
Total fat *1 g (2%)*
Saturated fat *None*
Protein *2 g*
Carbohydrate *36 g*
Cholesterol per serving
*None*
Vitamins *B₃*
Minerals *Potassium, Iron*

**6 oz pitted and chopped dates**
**1 tablespoon tamarind paste**
**1 tablespoon tomato ketchup**
**1 teaspoon ground coriander**
**1 teaspoon ground ginger**

**1 teaspoon chili powder**
**1 teaspoon sugar**
**1 tablespoon chopped fresh mint**
**salt**

**1**   Place all of the ingredients in a food processor with ⅔ cup water and salt to taste. Process for about 1-1½ minutes until smooth, stopping halfway through to scrape the mixture from the sides.
**2**   Transfer to a small bowl to serve. This chutney will keep for up to a week in the refrigerator.

# PANIR

SERVES 4

*This fresh cheese is an important ingredient in many Indian and Pakistani dishes. It is also often served as an extra dish, cut into cubes and swathed in a spicy tomato sauce like that for the Bombay Potatoes on page 132.*

PREPARATION
*about 10 minutes,
plus 1½-2 hours
setting*
COOKING
*about 20 minutes*

Calories per serving *116*
Total fat *4 g (31%)*
Saturated fat *3 g*
Protein *8 g*
Carbohydrate *13 g*
Cholesterol per serving
*18 mg*
Vitamins *B₂, B₃, B₆, B₁₂,
Folate*
Minerals *Calcium,
Potassium, Zinc, Iodine*

**4½ cups low-fat milk**

**2 tablespoons lemon juice**

**1**   Slowly bring the milk to a boil over low heat. Add the lemon juice, stirring continuously and gently until the milk thickens and begins to curdle. Strain the curdled milk through a sieve.
**2**   Set the strained curds aside between 2 chopping boards and put a heavy weight on top for 1½-2 hours to press them to a flat shape about ½ inch thick.
**3**   Once set, the panir can be cut like any cheese, into whatever shape is required.

*Slices of Panir served with Date and Tamarind Chutney, sliced red onion and mint sprigs*

# TOMATO AND ONION RAITA

SERVES 4

PREPARATION
*about 10 minutes*

Calories per serving *57*
Total fat *2 g (31%)*
Saturated fat *1 g*
Protein *5 g*
Carbohydrate *9 g*
Cholesterol per serving
*3 mg*
Vitamins $B_2$, $B_3$, $B_6B_{12}$,
*Folate*
Minerals *Calcium,*
*Potassium, Iron, Zinc,*
*Iodine*

*Raitas are served as accompaniments at most Indian meals, especially in northern India. This version is quite popular.*

1¼ cups low-fat plain yogurt
1 onion, diced
2 tomatoes, diced
2 fresh green chilies, diced
1 tablespoon chopped fresh cilantro leaves
about ½ teaspoon sugar

salt

for garnish:
pinch chili powder
pinch ground coriander

1  In a medium bowl, combine the yogurt, diced onion, tomatoes, green chilies, chopped cilantro, sugar, and salt to taste. Mix everything together well and transfer the raita to a serving dish.
2  Garnish with the chili powder and ground coriander, and serve.

# MINT AND MANGO RAITA

SERVES 4

PREPARATION
*about 20 minutes*

Calories per serving *82*
Total fat *1 g (9%)*
Saturated fat *1 g*
Protein *5 g*
Carbohydrate *15 g*
Cholesterol per serving
*3 mg*
Vitamins *A,* $B_2$, $B_3$, $B_6$,
*Folate, C*
Minerals *Calcium,*
*Potassium, Iodine*

*A traditional raita is made with yogurt, mint, cilantro, and cucumber. This unusual variation features mango and is one of my all-time favorites.*

1¼ cups low-fat plain yogurt
1 mango
1 fresh red chili, diced
1 teaspoon mint sauce
½ cucumber, sliced

1 tablespoon honey
2 tablespoons chopped fresh cilantro leaves
salt
mint leaves, for garnish (optional)

1  Whisk the low-fat yogurt well and place it in a serving bowl.
2  Peel the mango, cut it in half, and remove the pit (see page 24). Coarsely chop the flesh and place it in a food processor. Add the red chili, mint sauce, cucumber, honey, fresh cilantro, and salt to taste.

Process for about 1½ minutes, until the mixture is pulverized but not too smooth.
3  Add the mango mixture to the yogurt and gently stir together.
4  Garnish with mint leaves if you like, and serve.

*Mint and Mango Raita*

# COCONUT AND CILANTRO CHUTNEY

*Although fresh coconut is better, desiccated coconut may be substituted in this recipe.*

PREPARATION
*about 15 minutes*

Calories per serving *191*
Total fat *19 g (91%)*
Saturated fat *17 g*
Protein *2 g*
Carbohydrate *2 g*
Cholesterol per serving
*None*
Vitamins *B₃, C*
Minerals *Iron*

**scant 1½ cups grated fresh or desiccated coconut**
**1 fresh green chili, chopped**
**2 tablespoons chopped fresh mint**

**4 tablespoons chopped fresh cilantro leaves**
**salt**

**1** Place the coconut in a food processor and add the fresh green chili, chopped fresh mint, chopped fresh cilantro, and salt to taste. Process for about 2 minutes, stopping once to gather the mass together.

**2** Remove from the processor and transfer to a small serving bowl. Use within a day or two.

# MANGO AND COCONUT CHUTNEY

*As in the previous recipe, although it is best to use freshly grated coconut for this sweet-and-sour chutney, desiccated coconut will produce satisfying results.*

**1 large green mango**
**2 tablespoons chopped fresh cilantro leaves**
**2 fresh green chilies, chopped**
**1 tablespoon grated fresh or desiccated coconut**

**about 1 teaspoon sugar**
**salt**
**½ red bell pepper, seeded and chopped**

**1**  Peel the mango and discard the pit (page 24). Cut the mango flesh into small pieces.
**2**  Place the mango, cilantro, chilies, desiccated coconut, sugar, and salt to taste in a food processor. Process for about 1 minute or until everything is

quite finely chopped.
**3**  Pour in about ⅔ -1¼ cups water to achieve the consistency of a thick paste. Transfer to a serving dish and sprinkle with the chopped bell pepper.

PREPARATION
*about 20 minutes*

Calories per serving *52*
Total fat *3 g (43%)*
Saturated fat *2 g*
Protein *1 g*
Carbohydrate *7 g*
Cholesterol per serving
*None*
Vitamins *A, C*
Minerals *Potassium*

# QUICK MINT AND CUCUMBER RAITA

*It is surprising how easy it is to make this delicious raita, which is so versatile it can be served as an accompaniment to almost any meal.*

**½ cucumber**
**1¼ cups low-fat plain yogurt**
**salt**
**1 teaspoon sugar**

**1 teaspoon mint sauce**
**1 fresh red chili, diced**
**1 tablespoon chopped fresh cilantro leaves**
**fresh mint sprigs, for garnish**

**1**  Peel the cucumber and finely dice the flesh.
**2**  In a medium bowl, whisk the yogurt well. Add salt to taste, sugar, mint sauce, chili, and cilantro.

**3**  Add the cucumber and transfer to a serving bowl. Garnish with the mint sprigs to serve.

PREPARATION
*about 10 minutes*

Calories per serving *53*
Total fat *1 g (11%)*
Saturated fat *None*
Protein *4 g*
Carbohydrate *8 g*
Cholesterol per serving
*3 mg*
Vitamins $B_2$, $B_3$, $B_{12}$, *Folate*
Minerals *Calcium, Potassium, Iodine*

# Desserts

# TROPICAL FRUIT SALAD
# WITH ROASTED ALMONDS

SERVES 4

PREPARATION
*about 20 minutes,
plus roasting the
almonds*

Calories per serving *388*
Total fat *12 g (27%)*
Saturated fat *2 g*
Protein *9 g*
Carbohydrate *66 g*
Cholesterol per serving
*7 mg*
Vitamins *A, B group, C, E*
Minerals *Calcium,
Potassium, Iron, Zinc*

*2 large ripe mangoes*
*2 ripe papayas*
*3 ripe guavas (use canned if fresh are not
available)*
*8 black grapes, preferably seedless*
*8 white grapes, preferably seedless*
*1 Galia melon*
*1 small pineapple*

*2 bananas*
*1 red apple*
*2 fresh figs*
*2 kiwis*
*1 tablespoon confectioners' sugar*
*scant ½ cup almonds*
*1 cup low-fat fromage blanc (optional)*

*Previous pages: Tropical Fruit Salad with Roasted Almonds*

1   Prepare the fruit (try to save all the juices as you work): remove the flesh from the mangoes and discard the pits and skin (page 24). Slice the flesh coarsely. Cut the papayas in half and scoop out the seeds. Peel and cut the flesh into chunks. Seed the guavas if desired and scoop out chunks of flesh with a spoon. Place the fruit and juice in a serving bowl as it is ready.

2   Cut the grapes in half or leave them whole as you wish, and add to the bowl. Cut the melon in half and scoop out the seeds. Using a melon baller or sharp-sided spoon, scoop out balls and add to the bowl.

3   Pare the skin from the pineapple, halve, and remove the core. Slice thickly and then cut the slices into chunks and add to the bowl. Peel the bananas, slice them, and add to the bowl. Halve and core the apple, then cut into coarse chunks, and add to the bowl. Pour over any captured juices and toss lightly to mix.

4   Cut the figs in quarters. Peel and slice the kiwis. Place the kiwi slices and fig quarters on top of the fruit salad and dust with some confectioners' sugar. Chill briefly while you toast the almonds in a dry frying pan over moderate heat, turning frequently and taking care they do not burn, until they are well colored.

5   Serve the salad decorated with the roasted almonds and with the fromage blanc, if desired.

# BASIC RICE PUDDING

*Rice pudding is probably one of the most popular of Indian desserts, and most Indians make it on a regular basis at home.*

*½ cup basmati rice, well rinsed*
*5 cups low-fat milk*

*2 tablespoons desiccated coconut, plus more for decoration (optional)*
*6-8 tablespoons sugar*

1   Put the drained rice in a heavy-bottomed saucepan. Pour in half the milk and bring to a boil over moderate heat. Leave to boil gently for 12-14 minutes, until soft (a wooden spoon in the pan helps prevent the milk from boiling over).

2   When the rice is cooked, mash the rice down in the milk using a wooden masher, if possible; otherwise place half the rice in a food processor and process the rice down. Once the mixture is soft and mushy, add the coconut and blend in well.

3   Pour in the remaining milk and bring to a boil again. Cook at a gentle boil for 2-3 minutes, until it has the consistency of a thick creamy soup.

4   Stir in the sugar and cook, stirring, for an additional 2 minutes or so. Serve decorated with more desiccated coconut, if desired.

SERVES 4

PREPARATION
*5 minutes*
COOKING
*about 20 minutes*

Calories per serving *317*
Total fat *10 g (28%)*
Saturated fat *7 g*
Protein *12 g*
Carbohydrate *48 g*
Cholesterol per serving
*22 mg*
Vitamins *B₁, B₂, B₃, B₆, B₁₂,*
*Folate*
Minerals *Calcium,*
*Potassium, Zinc, Iodine*

# MANGO PULP WITH SAFFRON AND FROMAGE BLANC

*The taste of mangoes from the Indian subcontinent is quite something. The fruit is in season from around the middle of May until just before the monsoons at the end of July, and practically everyone looks forward to their arrival. Throughout the season, mangoes are prepared as desserts in many different ways.*

**4 large ripe mangoes**
**1¼ cups low-fat milk**
**heaping ½ cup low-fat fromage blanc**
**¼ teaspoon saffron threads**

**1 tablespoon sugar**
**1 oz mixed roasted sliced almonds and chopped pistachio nuts, for garnish (optional)**

1   Remove the flesh from the mangoes and discard the pits and skin (see page 24).

2   Place the mango flesh in a food processor together with the milk, fromage blanc, saffron, and sugar. Process until the mixture is smooth.

3   Transfer to a serving bowl and then decorate with the almonds and pistachio nuts, if desired.

# WATERMELON AND PAPAYA JUICE

*When I was a child, my mother would give us this refreshing juice on very hot days. Choose a watermelon with nice red flesh and a ripe but not overripe papaya.*

**1 small papaya**
**2 thick slices watermelon**
**1 tablespoon sugar**

**1 teaspoon lemon juice**
**6-8 ice cubes, crushed**

1   Cut the papaya in half and remove all the seeds. Peel the papaya and coarsely chop the flesh.

2   Remove the rind and as many seeds as possible from the watermelon. Chop the flesh coarsely.

3   Place the papaya, watermelon, sugar, and lemon juice in a blender with ½ cup water and process for 1-1½ minutes, until smooth.

4   Pour the juice through a sieve into glasses filled with crushed ice.

*Mango Pulp with Saffron and Fromage Blanc, Watermelon and Papaya Juice*

# RICE PUDDING WITH CARDAMOM AND SAFFRON

*For special occasions serve this rather special and delicately flavored rice pudding decorated with silver leaf.*

SERVES 4

PREPARATION
*about 10 minutes*
COOKING
*25-30 minutes*

Calories per serving *320*
Total fat *9 g (26%)*
Saturated fat *4 g*
Protein *14 g*
Carbohydrate *47 g*
Cholesterol per serving
*22 mg*
Vitamins *B₁, B₂, B₃, B₆, B₁₂, E*
Minerals *Calcium, Potassium, Iron, Zinc*

**3 tablespoons basmati rice**
**5 cups low-fat milk**
**green cardamom seeds from 1 cardamom pod**
**1 tablespoon ground almonds**
**6-8 tablespoons sugar**
**½ teaspoon saffron threads, lightly crushed**

**for garnish:**
**1 tablespoon sliced almonds**
**1 tablespoon ground pistachio nuts**
**silver leaf (optional)**

**1** Rinse the rice well, then put it in a large heavy-bottomed saucepan and add half the milk. Add the cardamom seeds and slowly bring to a boil over very low heat, stirring occasionally. Cook until all the milk has been absorbed by the rice, about 10 minutes, stirring occasionally.

**2** Remove from the heat and mash the rice, preferably using a wooden masher and making swift round movements, for at least 5 minutes.

**3** Return to the heat and add the ground almonds. Gradually stir in the remaining milk and bring to a boil, stirring occasionally.

**4** Add the sugar and stir for an additional 5-7 minutes, until the pudding is quite thick.

**5** Add the saffron threads and cook for an additional minute before transferring to a serving dish.

**6** Garnish with the sliced almonds, ground pistachio nuts, and silver leaf, if desired.

# SWEET POTATO DESSERT

*This delicious milky dessert can be eaten hot or cold.*

2 lbs sweet potatoes
3¾ cups low-fat milk

½ cup sugar
few sliced almonds, for garnish (optional)

1 Peel the sweet potatoes. Using a sharp knife, cut them into slices.

2 Place the sweet potato slices in a large saucepan, cover with 2½ cups milk, and cook slowly until the sweet potatoes are soft enough to be mashed.

3 Remove the pan from the heat and mash well, preferably with a wooden masher, with the milk in the pan to remove all the lumps.

4 Add the sugar and the remaining milk. Return to the heat and simmer gently until the mixture thickens. It should reach the consistency of a creamy soup.

5 Decorate with a few sliced almonds to serve, if desired.

SERVES 6-8

PREPARATION
*15 minutes*
COOKING
*about 20 minutes*

Calories per serving *207*
Total fat *2 g (10%)*
Saturated fat *1 g*
Protein *5 g*
Carbohydrate *44 g*
Cholesterol per serving
*7 mg*
Vitamins *A, B group, C, E*
Minerals *Calcium,
Potassium, Iodine*

# FRESH MANGO MILK SHAKE

*Try to find very ripe mangoes for this recipe.*

2 large ripe mangoes
sugar to taste

2½ cups low-fat or skim milk, plus more if necessary

1 Remove the flesh from the mangoes and discard the stones and skin (page 24). Slice the flesh coarsely.

2 Put the mango, milk, and sugar in a blender and process for 1-1½ minutes until thick and smooth. If it is too thick, add more milk.

3 Transfer to 2 or 3 glasses and serve chilled.

SERVES 2-3

PREPARATION
*about 15 minutes,
plus chilling*

Calories per serving *175*
Total fat *3 g (18%)*
Saturated fat *2 g*
Protein *7 g*
Carbohydrate *31 g*
Cholesterol per serving
*14 mg*
Vitamins *A, B group, C, E*
Minerals *Calcium,
Potassium, Iodine*

# MANGO AND PINEAPPLE JUICE DRINK

SERVES 2

PREPARATION
*about 15 minutes*

Calories per serving *132*
Total fat *1 g (4%)*
Saturated fat *None*
Protein *2 g*
Carbohydrate *33 g*
Cholesterol per serving
*None*
Vitamins *A, B₃, C, E*
Minerals *Potassium, Iron*

*The sweet rich flavor of the mango and the slight tang of the pineapple make this drink the perfect finish to a spicy meal.*

**2 large mangoes**
**½ pineapple**

**6-8 ice cubes, crushed**

1   Remove the flesh from the mangoes and discard the pits and skin (page 24). Dice the flesh coarsely.
2   Cut the pineapple flesh into cubes.
3   Place the fruit in a food processor or blender

with half the crushed ice. Process for 1-1½ minutes, until smooth. Stir in the remaining crushed ice and serve immediately.

# MANGO DRINK COCKTAIL

SERVES 2

PREPARATION
*about 10 minutes,*
*plus chilling*

Calories per serving *122*
Total fat *3 g (19%)*
Saturated fat *2 g*
Protein *5 g*
Carbohydrate *21 g*
Cholesterol per serving
*9 mg*
Vitamins *A, B₂, B₃, B₆,*
*B₁₂, C*
Minerals *Calcium,*
*Potassium, Iodine*

*This drink could easily pass for a dessert. Serve it either at the end of a meal or during the course of it. Canned mango pulp (if you can't find fresh mango) is available at most Asian stores.*

**6-8 ice cubes, crushed**
**2 tablespoons mango pulp**
**1 teaspoon lemon juice**
**⅔ cup low-fat plain yogurt**

**1 tablespoon sugar**
**2 tablespoons low-fat vanilla ice-cream**
**mint sprigs, for garnish (optional)**

1   Place the crushed ice in 2 tall glasses and chill in the refrigerator.
2   Mix together the mango pulp, lemon juice,

yogurt, sugar, and ice-cream.
3   Pour this mixture over the crushed ice and serve garnished with mint sprigs, if desired.

*Mango and Pineapple Juice Drink*

# CARDAMOM, PLUM, AND APRICOT DESSERT

SERVES 4

PREPARATION
*about 5 minutes*
COOKING
*20-25 minutes*

Calories per serving *173*
Total fat *2 g (12%)*
Saturated fat *1 g*
Protein *3 g*
Carbohydrate *37 g*
Cholesterol per serving
*7 mg*
Vitamins *A, B group*
Minerals *Potassium, Iron*

*5 ripe red plums*
*5 apricots*
*2 cardamom pods*
*¼ cup golden raisins*

*1 clove*
*4 tablespoons sugar*
*½ cup low-fat fromage blanc,*
*for serving (optional)*

1  Peel the plums and apricots, halve them and remove the pits.
2  Place the plums and apricots in a pan with the cardamom pods, raisins, clove, and sugar. Pour in 2½ cups water and stir well.

3  Bring to a boil, reduce the heat to moderate, and cook for 15-20 minutes, or until the fruit is tender and the water has become syrupy.
4  Allow to cool a little and serve warm, with the fromage blanc if you wish.

# ZAFRANI SEVIAN
## *Saffron Vermicelli Pudding*

SERVES 4

PREPARATION
*about 5 minutes*
COOKING
*about 30 minutes*

Calories per serving *224*
Total fat *5 g (21%)*
Saturated fat *2 g*
Protein *9 g*
Carbohydrate *38 g*
Cholesterol per serving
*15 mg*
Vitamins *B group*
Minerals *Calcium,*
*Potassium, Iodine*

*3¾ cups low-fat milk*
*3 tablespoons crushed fine vermicelli*
*large pinch saffron strands*

*2 tablespoons golden raisins*
*4 tablespoons sugar*
*1 tablespoon toasted flaked almonds*

1  Place the milk in a saucepan and add the vermicelli. Bring to a boil, then simmer gently for 15-20 minutes, until quite thick.
2  Stir in the saffron and simmer about 7 minutes more, stirring occasionally, until the mixture has

the consistency of a thick soup.
3  Stir in the raisins and sugar, and bring to a good rolling boil, briefly.
4  Transfer to a serving dish and serve decorated with the toasted almonds.

# INDEX

# ACKNOWLEDGMENTS

The author would like to express her grateful thanks to her mother for her continued support, her love for her husband, and many thanks to her children Humaira, Sumra, and Asim, wishing them all a long, happy, and healthy life.

Ameen

*Editor and Project Manager*: Lewis Esson
*Photographic Styling*: Antonia Gaunt
*Food Styling*: Janet Smith
*Nutritional Analysis*: Patricia Bacon
*Indexer*: Hilary Bird
*Page Make-up*: Clive Dorman & Co
*Production*: Peter Hinton
*Commissioning Editor*: Jo Christian
*Art Editor*: Louise Kirby
*Contributing Editor*: Sarah Mitchell
*Assistant Editor*: Kirsty Brackenridge
*Picture Editor*: Anne Fraser
*Editorial Director*: Erica Hunningher
*Art Director*: Caroline Hillier